LaVonne Neff

One of a Kind

Making the Most
of Your Child's Uniqueness

D0063954

MULTNOMAH

Portland, Oregon 97266

Edited by Liz Heaney
Cover design by Bruce DeRoos

ONE OF A KIND
© 1988 by LaVonne Neff
Published by Multnomah Press
Portland, Oregon 97266

Multnomah Press is a ministry of Multnomah School of the Bible,
8435 NE Glisan Street 97220

Printed in the United States of America

Library of Congress Cataloging-in-Publication Data

Neff, LaVonne.
One of a kind / by LaVonne Neff.
p.   cm.
Bibliography: p.
ISBN 0-88070-232-X (pbk.) : $8.95
1. Child rearing.   2. Child psychology.   3. Myers-Briggs Type Indicator.   I. Title.
HQ772.N43   1988
649'.1—dc19   88-10164
                                                              CIP

92   93   –   10   9   8   7   6   5   4   3   2

To my parents,

Norval and Blanche Pease,

living proof that you can be baffled
by your children and still do a fine job
raising them. I love you, Mom and Dad!

CONTENTS

Part One: Using Personality Type to Get to Know
Yourself and Your Children

1. It Takes All Kinds 13
2. Here's Looking at You 23
3. Alphabet Soup 29
4. Those Mysterious Introverts! 41
5. Finding Your Child's Type 51

Part Two: Using Personality Type to . . .

6. Find a Comfortable Parenting Style 65
7. Strengthen Your Marriage 77
8. Improve Family Communication 87
9. Discipline Your Children Effectively 99
10. Help Them Succeed in School 111
11. Give Them What They Need Most 121
12. Help Them Reach Their Full Potential 133
13. Lead Them Gently to God 145

Postscript   157

Appendix: Descriptions of the Sixteen Types   159

ESTJ	159	ISTJ	173
ENTJ	161	ISFJ	175
ESFJ	163	INTJ	177
ENFJ	165	INFJ	179
ESTP	166	ISTP	180
ESFP	168	INTP	182
ENTP	170	ISFP	184
ENFP	172	INFP	186

Bibliography of Books, Journals, and other
  MBTI Resources   189

Glossary   195

ACKNOWLEDGMENTS

For reading my manuscript, suggesting improvements, and helping me sift out inaccuracies and overstatement, I extend warm thanks in alphabetical order to Margaret Hartzler, Liz Heaney, Carrie C. Kulp, Gordon Lawrence, Mary H. McCaulley, Marcia Miller, David Neff, and Heidi Neff.

For offering hospitality and (sometimes endlessly) discussing type-related ideas, I am grateful to Joyce Blake, Ramona Cass, Gary Hartzler, Kathleen Mitchell, Molly Neff, Susan Scanlon, Adriana Serrano, John Testerman, Nancy Testerman, Adele Waller, Daryll Ward, and Adam Yagodtka.

The reader should realize that dominant intuitives never take every suggestion that comes their way, so none of the above persons should be blamed for any remaining errors. I put them in all by myself to keep the reader alert.

PART 1

CHAPTER 1

It Takes All Kinds

IF you are a parent, you know that seven-pound, fuzzy-topped babies are born equipped with highly individual personalities.

Some babies (so they say) sleep twenty-two hours a day and wake up smiling. Some sleep even less than the books recommend for a healthy adult—especially one who has just given birth. Some smile quickly at everyone, while others make sure it's really Mom before turning up the corners of their mouths. Some relax and cuddle, while others wiggle and squirm.

As babies grow into toddlers and preschoolers, the differences become even more apparent.

Steven, age three, was inadvertently left unguarded for perhaps two minutes while his mother and I were visiting in the living room. In that time he unrolled the toilet paper, emptied a can of talcum powder onto the rug, and reset the alarm clock.

I gave Caroline, a quite different three-year-old, a box of old toys to play with. She politely asked, "Is there something I should know about these toys before I touch them?"

Both children were bright, beloved, and being carefully brought up conscientiously. But their personalities were polar opposites.

Teachers are quick to pick up on children's personality differences. Several years later, when Steven entered kindergarten, his teacher could have sent this note home: "Steven is alert, curious, and enthusiastic. His mind is never still. He loves to investigate his world. He is a joy to have in class."

If she also had Caroline in class, she might have written: "Caroline is quiet and reserved. She often hangs back and does not join in group activities. It would be a good idea to encourage her to try new things and play with other children."

On the other hand, the teacher could just as easily have written quite different notes: "Steven finds it hard to sit still long enough to do his work sheets. He often annoys children seated next to him. He is inattentive and disruptive in class." Or to Caroline's parents: "Caroline is interested in her classwork. Her papers are always neat and on time. She is polite to me and to the other students. I wish more students were like her."

Why the different approaches to Steven and Caroline? Because teachers and parents, like children, come with varied personalities.

• Some of us love rushing in where angels fear to tread; others want to weigh each pro and con before taking the first step.

• Some overflow with ideas and possibilities; others are consistently sensible and practical.

• Some instinctively know how to relate to other people; others are gifted at analyzing and organizing.

• Some prefer learning; others prefer doing.

Ten Ways This Book Will
Help You Be a Better Parent

1. It will reveal your potential strengths as a parent.

2. It will explain why your parenting style should not be a carbon copy of your best friend's or your mother-in-law's.

3. It will tell why your spouse and children behave the way they do.

4. It will give you tools for strengthening your relationship with your spouse.

5. It will help you understand family members who keep their best side hidden.

6. It will teach you to speak so that your children listen.

7. It will help you train your children to discipline themselves.

8. It will show how to help your children make the most of their school experience.

9. It will reveal what your children most need from you.

10. It will show how to lead your little ones to God along the path he has prepared for them.

No Two Snowflakes Alike

People, like snowflakes, come in infinite varieties. We don't look, talk, think, feel, see, imagine, understand, act, decide, remember, or love just like anyone else. Each of us is unique, an original, a made-to-order creation. I, like you, have a God-given identity that is mine and mine alone.

"Thank goodness," a young mother said, "both my children aren't like Jennifer." She paused, then added, "Thank goodness they aren't both like Erik either!"

Jennifer and Erik, if they were old enough to talk, would no doubt complete their mother's thanksgiving: "Thank goodness both our parents aren't like Mom—or like Dad."

And indeed they all would be right. We should thank God that he created people with widely varying personalities, just as he created the world in living color. A family in which everyone behaved just like everyone else would be about as interesting as a world in which sky, grass, water, plants, animals, and human beings were all beige. Or chartreuse.

Personality differences, of course, can cause conflict. If some family members are scheduled and punctual while others are relaxed and often late, there will be many frustrations. The scheduled ones are unlikely ever to appreciate waiting, and the relaxed ones may not respond graciously when told to hurry up. Still, they may be healthier because of these differences. The family members will not risk turning into either scurrying ants or laid-back sloths. Their differences can give them balance and can actually make them appreciate one another all the more—if they do not become constant sources of misunderstanding, irritation, hurt, and open hostility.

Professor Higgins in *My Fair Lady* wondered, "Why can't a woman be more like a man?" The battle between the sexes was raging long before Ricky and Lucy, Fred and Ethel brought it to prime-time television, and many skirmishes involve personality differences. But husbands and wives, unlike brothers and sisters or parents and children, choose each other. Her light-hearted spontaneity draws him out of his overly serious ponderings. His visionary idealism sets fire to her practical, matter-of-fact nature. So they fall in love and marry.

No such matching occurs in the relationships formed when the children come along. It is very possible for two practical, orderly, decisive parents to produce a scatter-brained dreamer (and if you doubt this, I'll give you my parents' phone number). A gregarious, life-of-the-party parent can easily be given a child with the social interests of a Trappist monk; a methodical accountant may have to raise a beach bum; a fourteen-year-old who alphabetizes his underwear may have to share a bedroom with a twelve-year-old who collects birds' nests and never washes his socks.

Love and Exasperation

A recent study on motherhood concluded that a mother's feelings toward her child often have a lot to do with the way their personalities interact. This is hardly surprising. The same observation could be extended to other family relationships.

Gina, for example, is a quiet woman who enjoys an evening in front of the fireplace with a good book. She loves and admires her daughter, Sarah, an outgoing ten-year-old who usually brings at least three friends home from school every afternoon. Nevertheless, she is more comfortable with her eleven-year-old son, Mark, who can spend hours with his stamp collection or model airplanes.

Gina's sister is just the opposite. Angie is a joiner. She belongs to two clubs and four church groups, and she is a member of the library board, the school board, and a political action group. Angie often brags about her studious nephew, but when she comes to visit, it is bouncy Sarah she wants to see first.

When Angie and Gina were growing up, they shared a bedroom. Gina didn't often express her resentment to her younger sister, but she frequently felt invaded by Angie's friends, her loud music, her generally high noise level.

Now, whenever Angie and Sarah go out the door together laughing and chattering, Gina feels a stab of an old feeling she thought she had buried long ago. Is it resentment at their boisterousness? Is it envy of the good times they share? Is it a sense of injustice because Angie pays too little attention to Mark? Gina doesn't

know. She pushes the unwanted thought out of her con-
sciousness and goes into Mark's room to look at the model
schooner he has just begun assembling.

It's not hard to see that these family relationships
are colored by personality similarities and differences.
Gina is drawn toward Mark and away from Angie and
Sarah. Angie is drawn toward Sarah and away from Mark
and Gina. Yet all four of these people would die for each
other. They would like to understand what makes the
others tick. They would like to know themselves better.
But they don't know where to begin.

Personality Types

People have been observing personality differences
for thousands of years. The Greek physician Hippocrates,
four hundred years before Christ, spoke of four "humors"
that affected people's behavior and dispositions. In his
system, which was popular all through the Middle Ages,
a person's personality depended on the balance of blood,
phlegm, choler, and black bile in his or her body. The
names of Hippocrates' four temperaments are based on
the Latin words for the four humors: sanguine, phlegma-
tic, choleric, and melancholic.

"Humors" aren't taken seriously by modern
medicine, but Hippocrates gave us at least two important
insights. First, physical health inevitably affects the health
of the soul, the spirit, and the personality. Second, people
are different from one another in generally predictable
ways.

"The human race," someone has said, "is made up
of two groups of people: those who divide people into
groups, and those who don't." People who study personality development divide people into groups. Four has
been a popular number. It's easy to work with, and it
often works. Others use groupings of two, eight, nine,
sixteen. The number isn't important. What's important
is the enormous improvement in family happiness that

can result when the family members understand themselves and each other.

Most of us, being human, are reasonably content with who we are and find it hard to understand why others can't be like us. My mother, a wonderfully organized woman, often told me, "It takes more energy to throw your coat on the bed and hang it up later than to put it in the closet in the first place." She was absolutely right if she meant physical energy. She was right about mental energy, too, if she was talking about herself. But my personality is different from hers, and for me to direct my attention to hanging up coats when I was totally involved in some other project required an outlay of mental energy that my mother could not imagine.

My mother spent nineteen frustrating years trying to teach me to use her methods to be orderly. She then gave up and turned me over to my husband, who is not excessively orderly himself. Ten disorganized—even chaotic—years later, when I was pushing thirty, I finally developed my own system, my own methods. My mother is now able to come for an extended visit without even once throwing up her hands and exclaiming, "How can you live like this?"

But my methods of achieving my goal of having a reasonably clean house are different from hers because my personality is different. If we had understood those differences thirty years ago, we could have saved our selves a lot of gnashing of teeth.

And that is what this book is for—to save loving, well-intentioned parents unnecessary gnashing of teeth, weeping, shouting, and tearing out of hair as they bring up their bright, darling, and unique offspring.

The Myers-Briggs Type Indicator

In this book I will often mention the Myers-Briggs Type Indicator (MBTI), an excellent tool for understanding ourselves and our loved ones.[1] The MBTI is widely available. It is easy to understand. It deals with significant personality differences. Besides, it is popular.

An interest in the MBTI is sweeping the business world, where it is used to improve management style, team building, job satisfaction, and relationships among coworkers.

The MBTI is becoming well known in churches and religious communities, where it helps people in their personal spiritual growth, approach to prayer, development of spiritual gifts, and relationships with other members of Christ's body.

The MBTI is being widely used by marriage and family counselors to help people understand each other, communicate more effectively, and use their differences constructively.

With over a million people filling out the MBTI every year, it is taking the country by storm.

Riding the subway in suburban Washington, D. C., during the afternoon rush hour, I was reading the latest copy of *The Type Reporter* (a quarterly publication on psychological type). A man sat down next to me, looked over my shoulder at what I was reading, and said, "I'm an ENTP—who are you?"

He was using a language familiar to "typewatchers"—people who are interested in how personality type affects behavior—to introduce himself, and I laughingly gave him my letters, ENFP. If an uninitiated person stumbles into a roomful of typewatchers, he or she may be taken aback by the odd vocabulary. ISFJ. ENTJ. INTP. The S-function. The E-orientation. As one man lamented, "My wife went to a weekend conference and came back speaking in alphabets."

Don't be alarmed. You can be sure that the hundreds of thousands of people in this country who already know their MBTI personality type did not go to grad school in their spare time to learn about it. Instead, they picked up their knowledge from books, from church-sponsored conferences, from training seminars where they work.

Personality type is not difficult to understand. Although you may enjoy playing with the system for the rest of your life, you can begin to get a working knowledge of it in less than an hour. It is clear. It is logical. It is immensely helpful in understanding and dealing with those closest to us. It can make you a more effective parent.

Begin by figuring out your own personality type, either by taking the MBTI or by taking the quiz in chapter 2. Then, if you are the kind of person who likes step-by-step explanations given in logical order, keep reading straight through the book.

On the other hand, if you are the kind of person who prefers jumping immediately into practical applications, you may want to turn to Part 2 and see how to use personality type to accomplish your most pressing goals.

Or maybe you already have the general idea in mind and would prefer reading the book in your own idiosyncratic order—first the appendix, perhaps, and then chapter 12 (if it catches your eye), followed by a quick dip into chapter 4 to clarify a point you didn't quite understand. If this is your style, you may not even be reading this now—but that's okay. Read it your way.

You see, you can't escape personality differences, especially not when reading a book about them!

1. Katharine C. Briggs and Isabel Briggs Myers, *Myers-Briggs Type Indicator* (Palo Alto, Calif.: Consulting Psychologists Press, 1977).

CHAPTER 2

Here's Looking at You

FLIGHT attendants direct parents, in cases of emergency, to fasten their own oxygen masks before helping their children fasten theirs. Likewise, it's important to find out your own personality type before trying to decide your children's.

It is important to know your own personality type *as well as* your children's types because families are systems of relationships, not collections of isolated individuals. Personality type would be irrelevant if we each lived alone on our own desert islands. Whether we were reserved or sociable, hard-driving or relaxed would matter little to the monkeys and tortoises. If you look at your children's types without looking at yours, you will have information with no possibility of application. You will not know how your personalities affect your relationships.

It is important to know your own personality type *before* looking at your children's types because type is intensely personal. You are the world's foremost authority on your own personality type. If you fill out a type questionnaire, *you* provide the answers. When you get your type report, *you* say if it is accurate or not. Until you have had the experience of identifying your own type, you are unlikely to do a good job of identifying someone else's.

How then can you find out your personality type? There are many possible approaches (see the suggestions on page 27). The best way is to take the Myers-Briggs Type Indicator, a thoroughly researched and validated psychological instrument that is given to well over a million people every year.

If you can't find a way to take the MBTI in your community, however, or if you don't want to wait until you've taken it to begin learning about type, here's a quiz to get you started.

WORD CHOICE QUIZ

Here are thirty-six word pairs. In most cases, one word of each pair will seem more like your style than the other word.

Number a sheet of paper from 1 to 36. (It will be easier to find your score if you make two columns, just as the word pairs are given.) Write down the letter of the word you prefer in each pair.

As soon as they take the MBTI or some other personality type indicator, most people look immediately for a description of their own type. Then as soon as they've digested it, they try to locate their spouse, their children, their impossible boss, their friends.

You can do that, too. In the appendix you'll find a short description of each of the sixteen types.

Does your description fit you? If so, write your four letters in the front of this book so you won't forget them. If not, read other descriptions until you find one that sounds more like you.

1. a. people
   b. places

2. a. structure
   b. freedom

3. a. forest
   b. trees

4. a. mercy
   b. justice

5. a. reflect
   b. act

6. a. organized
   b. flexible

7. a. broad
   b. deep

8. a. curious
   b. decisive

9. a. facts
   b. possibilities

10. a. head
    b. heart

11. a. observant
    b. imaginative

12. a. enthusiastic
    b. consistent

13. a. party
    b. library

14. a. plan
    b. improvise

15. a. theoretical
    b. practical

16. a. question
    b. answer

17. a. private
    b. public

18. a. work
    b. play

19. a. write
    b. speak

20. a. cool
    b. warm

21. a. city
    b. forest

22. a. manager
    b. entrepreneur

23. a. contented
    b. restless

24. a. truth
    b. tact

25. a. production
    b. design

26. a. order
    b. harmony

27. a. look
    b. leap

28. a. values
    b. logic

29. a. insightful
    b. sensible

30. a. fair
    b. kind

31. a. change
    b. conserve

32. a. start
    b. finish

33. a. tortoise
    b. hare

34. a. relational
    b. analytical

35. a. discuss
    b. consider

36. a. process
    b. outcome

KEY

1. After each number, circle the letter of the answer you chose.

2. For each vertical column (E, I, S, etc.), count the number of circled letters and write the total in the space provided below.

3. Notice that the vertical columns are arranged in four groups of two: E/I, S/N, T/F, and J/P. Take the letter with the highest total in each group and write it at the bottom of the chart ("My Personality Type Code"). For example, if you circled 3 E-answers and 6 I-answers, write an I in the first space.

4. To understand what your four-letter code means, keep reading this book!

	E	I	S	N		T	F	J	P
1.—a	b				2.———a	b			
3.————b	a				4.——b	a			
5.—b	a				6.————a	b			
7.—a	b				8.————b	a			
9.————a	b				10.—a	b			
11.————a	b				12.—b	a			
13.—a	b				14.————a	b			
15.————b	a				16.————b	a			
17.—b	a				18.————a	b			
19.—b	a				20.—a	b			
21.—a	b				22.————a	b			
23.————a	b				24.—a	b			
25.————a	b				26.—a	b			
27.—b	a				28.—b	a			
29.————b	a				30.—a	b			
31.————b	a				32.————b	a			
33.————a	b				34.—b	a			
35.—a	b				36.————b	a			

TOTALS

(E: ___ I: ___) S: ___ N; ___) (T: ___ F: ___) (J: ___ P: ___)

MY PERSONALITY TYPE CODE: ___ ___ ___ ___
     (E/I) (S/N) (T/F) (J/P)

Five Ways to Find Out Your Personality Type

1. The Most Accurate Way

Fill out the Myers-Briggs Type Indicator (MBTI). To find out who gives it in your area, ask your pastor, the local ministerial association, or a counseling center. Or you can contact the Association for Psychological Type (APT), P. O. Box 5099, Gainesville, FL 32602, 904/371-1853, and they will put you in touch with a type-users' group near you.

2. The Quickest Way

Take the Word Choice Quiz in chapter 2. It is not a scientifically researched measuring instrument like the MBTI, and research findings about the MBTI will not necessarily apply to the Word Choice Quiz. Still, it can provoke your thinking, start discussion, and help you understand the concept of personality types.

3. The Experiential Way

After taking the MBTI or the Word Choice Quiz and obtaining a four-letter code, look in the Appendix to find the description that matches that code. Does it fit you pretty well? Read descriptions of types that are similar. Do any of them fit you better? When you find a type description that seems to describe you, show it to your spouse, your older children, your friends, your parents. Do they agree that it sounds like you? If you are wavering between types, ask them to help you choose.

4. The Sociable Way

Look for a weekend seminar on personality type. Often held in church basements on Saturdays, these can be located through your pastor, ministerial association, or counseling center. Or call your local newspaper office to see if announcements of forthcoming seminars have been sent in.

5. The Studious Way

This book is an introduction to personality type theory, emphasizing its importance to parents and children. Don't stop here. Read other books on type and temperament. Three of the best known are *Gifts Differing*, by Isabel Briggs Myers; *Please Understand Me*, by David Keirsey and Marilyn Bates; and *People Types and Tiger Stripes*, by Gordon Lawrence. Full information on these and other books is given in the bibliography.

But what do the letters mean? To describe the observable differences in people's personalities, Katharine Briggs and Isabel Myers took terms used by Swiss psychologist C. G. Jung and assigned a letter to each term. Your letters are a shorthand description of four aspects of your personality. Chapter 3 explains each of the eight letters in detail.

CHAPTER 3

Alphabet Soup

Now you have an idea of what your four-letter code might be. You seem to be an ISTJ, ISFJ, INFJ, INTJ, ISTP, ISFP, INFP, INTP, ESTP, ESFP, ENFP, ENTP, ESTJ, ESFJ, ENFJ, or ENTJ. But what do the letters mean?

Each of the eight letters stands for a personality characteristic.

E = Extraversion ———————— I = Introversion
S = Sensing ———————————— N = Intuiting
T = Thinking ——————————— F = Feeling
J = Judging ———————————— P = Perceiving

The first pair of letters, E and I, tell whether a person orients himself or herself toward the outer world or toward inward reality. E and I are sometimes called *attitudes*.

The second pair, S and N, tell how a person perceives or gathers information. S and N are *functions* or processes.

The third pair, T and F, tell how a person judges or

makes decisions about information. Like S and N, T and F are *functions*.

The fourth pair, J and P, tell whether the person prefers to perceive or to judge in the outer world. J and P are sometimes called *orientations*.

In each of the four pairs of traits, we tend to prefer one trait over the other. Thus we end up with one attitude (represented by the first letter of our code), two functions (represented by the two middle letters), and one orientation. Don't worry about attitudes and functions and orientations at this point. If you need to brush up on them later, you can turn back to this page or check them out in the glossary at the back of the book.

Extraversion and Introversion

The letter E means a preference for the extraverted attitude over the introverted attitude. If extraversion is your preferred attitude, you are generally more comfortable when you focus your energy on the outer environment. You are often interested in people, things, and activity around you. The letter I, by contrast, indicates a preference for introversion. If that's your preferred attitude, you are usually more comfortable when you focus your energy on the inner world. You are often interested in ideas, thoughts, and reflection.

No matter whether your first letter is E or I, you extravert your energy part of the time and introvert your energy part of the time. You really have no choice. To survive you have to relate to the environment. To be fully human you have to take time to think and reflect.

When you say, "I'm an extravert," all you mean is that you are more comfortable in the outer world than in the inner world. When you say, "My child is an introvert," all you mean is that he or she is more at ease in the inner world than in the outer world.

It's like being right-handed or left-handed. Most people are born favoring one hand over the other. When

Eight Misunderstandings about Personality Type

In talking about personality type, Jung used common German words in a rather specialized way. Myers and Briggs took the English translations of these words and also used them in a way that is not always the same as their usual meaning.

Some people misunderstand the MBTI because they think of the terms in their usual sense, not their special sense. (Note: These eight traits are grouped into four pairs: 1-2, 3-4, etc. Each of us will be more comfortable with one of the traits in each of the four pairs.)

1. An EXTRAVERT *is not* necessarily a back-slapping party animal. He or she *is* a person who draws energy from interacting with the outer world of people or things.

2. An INTROVERT *is not* necessarily a hermit in a cave deep in the forest. He or she *is* a person who draws energy from making contact with the inner world of concepts and ideas.

3. A SENSING TYPE *is not* necessarily sensible, sensitive, or sensual. He or she *is* a person who enjoys perceiving the world through the five senses.

4. An INTUITIVE TYPE *is not* necessarily a prophet, a poet, or a woman. He or she *is* a person who enjoys perceiving the world by quickly jumping from sensory impressions into possibilities, associations, and symbols.

5. A THINKING TYPE *is not* necessarily unemotional, scholarly, or even unusually bright. He or she *is* a person who prefers making decisions on the basis of consistent, logical analysis.

6. A FEELING TYPE *is not* necessarily illogical, irrational, or even particularly emotional. He or she *is* a person who prefers making decisions on the basis of personal values.

7. A JUDGING TYPE *is not* necessarily judgmental. He or she *is* a goal-oriented person who likes to live in a planned and orderly way.

8. A PERCEIVING TYPE *is not* necessarily perceptive. He or she *is* a process-oriented person who likes to remain open to new information, insights, and experiences.

I use my right hand, I am comfortable, quick, and confident. When I use my left hand for a right-handed task, I am awkward and slow. But that doesn't tempt me to chop off my left hand. I need it to give me balance, to assist my right hand, to take over when my right hand is temporarily out of service. In fact, if I lost my left hand through an accident, I would feel quite handicapped. Both hands are necessary for smooth functioning.

Likewise, I need both extraversion and introversion. I need to be able to deal effectively with the world around me, and I need to be aware of my inner insights, experiences, thoughts, and feelings. Still, I will be more comfortable with one side than the other.

This is a right-handed society, as my left-handed husband can attest. The vast majority of books, scissors, mugs, and calligraphy pens are designed for the convenience of the right-hander and the frustration of the left-hander. As a result, David has learned to perform many tasks with his right hand: combing his hair, brushing his teeth, playing racquetball. He is much more skilled at using his right hand than I am at using my left.

A similar thing happens with some personality traits. America is geared to extraverts. It has been estimated that more than two-thirds of us are extraverts, less than one-third introverts. To get along in our fast-paced, action-oriented society, a person who prefers introversion has to develop extraversion as well. David, who is not only left-handed but also introverted, values time alone. Nevertheless, he has learned to greet a roomful of people, interview VIPs, and solicit for the American Cancer Society. Introverts, in fact, are often better at extraverting than extraverts at introverting. They have to be, to survive.

Note that this definition of extraversion and introversion does not assess social skill or shyness. An extravert is a person who gets energy from the outer environment and by contrast becomes restless or tired when forced to pay too much attention to the inner world. This does not mean, however, that every extravert is skillful in dealing with others.

Conversely, an introvert is a person who gets energy from deep within and feels depleted when forced to pay too much attention to the external environment. This does not mean that introverts necessarily lack friendliness or social skills.

Although extraverts, because they usually spend so much time dealing with others, often are friendly and sociable, they are not always the life of the party. Similarly, even though introverts, because they focus their attention within, may neglect the outer world and feel hesitant when they must deal with it, they are not always bashful and retiring. Extraverts can be shy, and introverts can be socially adept. Many are.

Sensing and Intuition

Your second letter, S (Sensing) or N (iNtuition), tells how you *perceive* the world, how you gather information. Thus MBTI users call sensing and intuition *perceiving functions*.

All of us perceive the world through our senses, of course. We see, hear, touch, taste, and smell. People who prefer to perceive through sensing enjoy the impressions they receive, and they focus on them. Blazing autumn colors; the ping caused by low-octane gas; a two-degree drop in temperature; real butter on homemade bread; a dirty sneaker left under the bed—sensing types notice these things.

People who prefer to perceive through sensing tend to be observant. This helps them if they happen to be Indian scouts, spies, reporters, or grade school teachers (with eyes in the back of their heads).

Sensing types usually pay attention to detail. This makes them effective accountants, secretaries, tailors, or pharmacists.

Sensing types are often good natured. Oriented to

present experience, they see no reason to brood over the past or—especially—to try to project the future. Quite contented to live in the here and now, they understand Matthew 6:34: "Do not worry about tomorrow, for tomorrow will worry about itself. Each day has enough trouble of its own."

Because of their way of perceiving the world, people who prefer sensing often pride themselves on being practical, matter-of-fact, down to earth, realistic. They are the people we think of when we hear terms like "salt of the earth" and "pillars of the church." Perhaps three-fourths of all Americans are sensing types.

But not everyone prefers to perceive the world through sensing. A solid minority would rather process it through intuition. These people use their senses, of course—if they didn't, they wouldn't be human. But when their eyes, ears, nose, tongue, or skin tells them something, they turn the information into a jumping-off point.

Instead of concentrating on the soup he is stirring, an intuitive cook may be dreaming of the soup-and-salad restaurant he could open. Instead of savoring the pungent October smell of burning leaves, the intuitive engineer may be mentally devising a non-polluting leaf-disposal method. Instead of merely keeping track of the details of his boss's forthcoming travel plans, the intuitive assistant may be trying to find her better accommodations at smaller cost.

Give a Noah's Ark set to a sensing child, and she will probably learn the names of each animal, admire their colors and facial expressions, line them up neatly next to the Ark, and play games in which they enter the Ark in matched pairs.

Give the same Noah's Ark to an intuitive child, and she may do anything with it. Yes, she will use her senses enough to know that it is an Ark with four little men, four little women, and twelve pairs of animals. But this may not matter much to her. She may decide to play church with her friends, pass the Ark around as a collection plate, and distribute little animals to be dropped in as the plate is passed. Later the Ark may turn into a salad bowl, and elephants and tigers into tomatoes and olives.

People who prefer to gather information through intuition often pay scant attention to the here and now, the actual, the facts. Instead, they are tuned in to the future, the possible, their inspirations. Intuitive types are often seen as creative, innovative, and imaginative. Because they are always looking for a better—or at least a different—approach, however, they may be restless or even discontented.

A sensing type might enjoy the dazzling description of the New Jerusalem in Revelation 21:10-27, with its profusion of precious stones, gold, glass, and pearls. An intuitive type would probably prefer 1 Corinthians 2:9: "No eye has seen, no ear has heard, no mind has conceived what God has prepared for those who love him." What an invitation to let the imagination play!

Thinking and Feeling

In addition to the two perceiving functions (sensing and intuition), there are also two *judging functions*. Your third letter, T (thinking) or F (feeling), tells how you *judge* the world. Before that sentence makes any sense, three terms have to be defined.

Judging is a way of acting on information that has been perceived. It means making decisions, setting priorities, choosing, and valuing.

Thinking is a way of judging (decision making) based on logical analysis, principles, policy, and justice.

Feeling is a way of judging (decision making) based on personal values, ideals, individual needs, and mercy.

Everyone uses a combination of thinking and feeling. Some circumstances call for one; some for the other; some for both. About sixty percent of men and forty percent of women are more comfortable basing their decisions on thinking. About forty percent of men and sixty percent of women are more comfortable basing their decisions on feeling.

Thinking and *feeling* are loaded words. They can easily become labels used to denigrate people we don't completely understand. "You have no feeling!" and "Why don't you try thinking?" are not statements that build up relationships.

As a matter of fact, thinking types can be just as emotional as feeling types. Feeling types can think just as clearly as thinking types. To say that you prefer thinking-judgment simply means you like to base your choices on objective analysis. It does not rule out a rich emotional life. To say that you prefer feeling-judgment simply means you like to base your choices on subjective values. The feeling process of making decisions is as rational as the thinking process.

A feeling child is often concerned for harmony. He wants to be liked, and he wants other family members to like each other. If a lie will keep the peace, he may be tempted to tell it.

A thinking child is often concerned for truth. She simply will not accept "Because I said so" as a reason for compliance. Her favorite question is "Why?"

A person who prefers feeling-judgments usually functions better if she knows she is appreciated. A word of genuine praise from her boss, her husband, her friends, her children can motivate her better than any other incentive.

A person who prefers thinking-judgments usually functions better if he believes he is being treated fairly. He may not be moved by praise; he may even be suspicious of it. But if he thinks he is being treated inequitably, watch out.

Notice how sensing and intuition, thinking and feeling work together if I am making a decision.

First, I must *perceive* the situation. I may do this

largely through *sensing* by making observations and noting details. Or I may do this largely through *intuition* by looking at how the facts relate or at the possibilities they point to.

Second, I must *judge* the situation. I may base my decision on *thinking* by analyzing the situation and applying objective principles, policies, or laws to it. Or I may base it on *feeling* by putting myself into the situation and applying subjective values and sympathetic understanding to it.

If my personality is well balanced and the situation calls for it, I may use all four of my functions—sensing, intuition, thinking, feeling—to perceive and judge. Through sensing I gather data; through intuition I look for possibilities; through thinking I apply principles; through feeling I evaluate what's important to me and those I love. Even if I do this, though, I will still find some functions easier to use than others. In my case, intuiting is more natural than sensing; feeling is more comfortable than thinking. My father is just the opposite—and yet we usually agree with and respect each other's decisions.

Judging and Perceiving

By now you are well acquainted with the terms *judging* (J) and *perceiving* (P), one of which is represented by your fourth letter. This fourth letter represents an *orientation*. It tells how you orient yourself to the outer world: whether with your perceiving function or with your judging function.

For example, if your fourth letter is P, you tend to run your outer life with your perceiving function. The two possible ways of perceiving, as you recall, are sensing and intuiting. These are both ways of taking in information about the world. Thus a person who prefers perceiving loves to gather information.

If your fourth letter is J, you run your outer life

with your judging function. The two possible ways of judging, of course, are thinking and feeling. These are both ways of making decisions about the world. Thus a person who prefers judging loves to make decisions.

Because this fourth letter, J or P, represents your way of acting in the world, your preference will most likely be quite obvious to people who know you.

If you prefer judging, you are likely to be in control, decisive, structured, and productive. You like to make lists and plans; you may enjoy being in charge; you want things done efficiently and purposefully. People may see you as self-disciplined or strong-willed. If you are a manager or administrator and like your work, your fourth letter is probably J.

If your fourth letter is J, you may like to make decisions as quickly as possible, to get matters settled and out of the way without dilly-dallying around. Thus if you have a weakness, it may be that you jump to conclusions without adequately perceiving the issues involved. Carried to extremes, this may lead to prejudice. The Pharisees that Jesus characterized as "blind guides" (Matthew 23:16) were probably unbalanced judging types.

If, on the other hand, you prefer perceiving, you are likely to be curious, flexible, process oriented, and adaptable. You enjoy surprises, and you may be very good at handling the unexpected. You love learning, and you tend to get interested in new projects and experiences. People may see you as a person of wide interests or great enthusiasm. If you enjoy a succession of new projects and new experiences, your fourth letter is probably P.

If your fourth letter is P, you may resist making decisions because you never feel as if you have enough information. Thus if you have a weakness, it may be that you let opportunities slip through your fingers. Carried to extremes, this may lead to irresponsibility. The apostle Paul described some unbalanced perceiving types as "always learning but never able to acknowledge the truth" (2 Timothy 3:7).

Some people misunderstand the meaning of *judging* and *perceiving*. Not realizing that these terms refer to the way we take in information and the way we act on it, they think the terms mean "judgmental" and "perceptive." This is not true. It is quite possible for either a judging type or a perceiving type to be judgmental. Both judgers and perceivers are often perceptive. Keep in mind that MBTI terms carry special meanings that may or may not correspond with the general public's understanding of the same or similar words (see "Eight Misunderstandings about Personality Type," page 31).

Occasionally a person who prefers to interact with the world through judging will begin acting in a totally off-the-wall way, or a person who prefers to interact through perceiving will become unusually decisive and even dictatorial. This may simply mean that the person is taking a vacation from his or her usual way of interacting—and there's no harm in doing that from time to time.

On the other hand, if the person is an introvert, it may mean something much more significant. Introverts are fascinating people. To explain their sometimes surprising behavior, we need a separate chapter.

CHAPTER 4

Those Mysterious Introverts!

SARAH, age eleven, is a quiet child. She is usually polite and pleasant and often does favors for others. She hardly ever resists, argues, or talks back to her parents. She rarely fights with her brother and sister. In fact, when they quarrel with each other, she tries to restore harmony.

Sarah's parents were astounded when one Sunday after church, Sarah's Sunday school teacher asked to talk with them privately. "I'm not sure how to handle Sarah," he said. "Most of the time she simply won't pay attention. She whispers to the other kids and keeps them from listening, too. And if she does listen, it's even worse—she attacks everything I say."

If the Sunday school teacher hadn't been a family friend, Sarah's parents would have wondered if he was talking about another girl. Mystified, they promised to speak with their daughter.

"I can't stand him," was her initial response.

"But we've known him for years," her parents

countered. "Besides, even if you don't like him you should respect him."

"Maybe I should," Sarah said, "but what he says is wrong. I won't listen to it, and I don't think the other kids should listen either."

As it turned out, the trouble began when Sarah's teacher presented a lesson on hell. He did not put the doctrine of punishment in the context of God's love and grace. Instead, he talked of eternally writhing spirits and everlastingly gnawing worms in terms that would have made Jonathan Edwards shudder.

Initially, Sarah was terrified. Then she put her teacher's words together with what her parents and other teachers had already told her of God's longing that all might be saved. If God was anything like her father, Sarah thought, he could not be like the executioner described by her Sunday school teacher.

And Sarah went to battle against what she saw as the forces of evil—not the devil this time, but her Sunday school teacher.

Dr. Jekyll and Mr. Hyde?

Did an unwise teacher shake introverted Sarah into a totally different personality group? Not at all. Sarah was acting true to her type—ISFP.

The characteristics of each of the preferences cannot be completely understood in isolation from each other. You may know all there is to know about extraverts and introverts, sensing types and intuiting types, thinkers and feelers, judgers and perceivers and still not realize what happens when four of these characteristics interact.

Sarah is definitely introverted. Because her fourth letter is P, she usually shows the outer world her perceiving function: sensing. People think of Sarah as practical, matter-of-fact, and realistic. They appreciate her for being obedient and compliant.

Two Ways to Find Out Your Dominant Function
(besides looking it up in the appendix)

Note: In MBTI terminology, your *functions* are represented by your second and third letters. Sensing, intuiting, thinking, and feeling are the four functions. One of these is dominant.

1. The take-it-by-faith way

>Write your four letters here: _____ _____ _____ _____
>Check the statement that describes your letters:
>
>_____ A. My first letter is E and my fourth letter is J
>_____ B. My first letter is I and my fourth letter is P
>_____ C. My first letter is E and my fourth letter is P
>_____ D. My first letter is I and my fourth letter is J

If you checked A or B, your dominant function is represented by your third letter, T or F. If you checked C or D, your dominant function is represented by your second letter, S or N. My dominant function is probably _____.

2. The figure-it-out way

A. My second letter is _____. It tells how I *perceive*—how I take in information about the world.

B. My third letter is _____. It tells how I *judge*—how I make decisions and why I move into action.

C. My fourth letter is _____. It tells which side of me is more obvious to other people. If it is J, I tend to show the world my way of judging: either thinking or feeling. If it is P, I tend to show the world my way of perceiving: either sensing or intuition. I prefer to show the world my _____
_____.

D. My first letter is _____. It tells whether I am more comfortable in the external world or the internal world.
If it is E, I am more comfortable with the side of me that I show other people. My dominant function, then, is the one I show the world.

If it is I, I am more comfortable with the side of me that I keep to myself. My dominant function, then, is the one I *do not* typically show the world.

My dominant function is probably _____.

She does not often show the world her judging function: feeling. She keeps this to herself. But *because she is an introvert, the function she keeps to herself is more important to her than the function she shows the world.*

A person is using the feeling function whenever he or she uses personal values to discriminate between right and wrong, wise and unwise. One of Sarah's most deeply held values is her personal relationship to God, whom she sees as an infinitely loving, tender, caring Father. Many of Sarah's decisions flow from this value. For example, one reason she obeys her parents and follows the rules of her church is that she believes this will please her heavenly Father.

When Sarah's Sunday school teacher presented a contradictory picture of God, Sarah was shattered. Her loving Father would not enjoy tormenting people! He would not spend even two seconds devising means of making people miserable for eternity! Her teacher must be wrong—and maybe worse than that. He must be guilty of telling lies about God.

If Sarah had been an adult, she might have found quiet, behind-the-scenes ways to remove the man from his teaching position. But Sarah was only eleven. She could not complain about him to her parents; he was their friend. She knew of no other indirect way to challenge his authority except simply to tune him out. So that is what she did, until he insisted that she pay attention. And then peace-loving Sarah could stand his challenge to her values no longer. She attacked.

What You See May Not Be What You Get

Introverts are always full of surprises. By their very nature, they keep their most preferred side hidden. You can be an introvert's spouse or parent and think you know him or her very well, and suddenly he or she does something completely unexpected.

A normally mild-mannered introverted feeling type

(ISFP, INFP) like Sarah may unexpectedly stand up for a cherished belief. He or she may challenge authority, give impassioned speeches, even lead a movement.

Similarly, a usually taciturn introverted thinking type (ISTP, INTP), if his or her principles are violated, may drop the compliant exterior and let the world see the firm, decisive, unyielding thinking underneath.

Introverts whose fourth letter is J tend to be organized and orderly. Their lives may seem well planned and to a perceiving type, even boring—unless they feel comfortable enough to unbar the gates and let others into their inner castles.

An off-duty introverted intuitive type (INTJ, INFJ), though usually the image of hard-working responsibility, turns out to have a vast, rich, chaotic imagination.

Likewise, an introverted sensing type (ISTJ, ISFJ), normally the most duty-bound of all, throws off shoes and overcoat and reveals a wacky sense of humor.

Because introverts keep their preferred side hidden, their fourth letter—J or P—does not tell the whole story about them. Yes, introverts who conduct their outer lives with judging are usually orderly planners—but occasionally their hidden sensing or intuition may well up and spill over into their public worlds.

Yes, introverts who conduct their outer lives with perceiving are usually agreeable and compliant—but occasionally their hidden thinking or feeling may stamp its figurative foot and refuse to budge.

Whenever the dominant function—the function introverts normally keep inside—comes out in public, the introvert seems to change personality.

Understanding the Dominant Function

Compared to introverts, extraverts are easy to understand. By definition they are comfortable in the external environment. They would rather interact with people and things than delve into their inner selves. Thus they show the world the side of themselves they prefer the most—their dominant function.

(A brief review: a *function* is a way of judging or perceiving. There are four functions. The perceiving functions are sensing and intuition. The judging functions are thinking and feeling. People tend to prefer one perceiving function and one judging function. Of these two preferred functions, one will be dominant.)

If an extravert prefers to live in a relaxed, casual manner, he or she shows the perceiving function: either sensing or intuition. If an extravert chooses to live in a planned, organized manner, he or she shows the judging function: either thinking or feeling. Whatever function the extravert shows is the function the extravert values the most. It is his or her dominant function. It is in charge.

Of course extraverts also have an interior side. A perceiving extravert keeps a judging function inside. A judging extravert keeps a perceiving function inside. But these functions are auxiliary, not dominant. They are unlikely to rise up and overwhelm the outer function, because the outer function is dominant. (It is just the reverse with the introvert, in whom the inner function is dominant and therefore may at any time decide to take over.)

You don't need to do mental gymnastics to understand an extravert, even if the extravert is only three years old. What you see is what you get. If you deal only with extraverts, understanding the theory of the dominant function may be interesting but relatively unimportant.

Most of us, however, deal with both extraverts and introverts. Since introverts are in the minority, they are easily overlooked or misunderstood—especially because they rarely toot their own horns. If there is even one introverted person in your family, you need to be sure you understand how the dominant function may make this person behave.

More Alphabet Soup

Keep in mind that a person's fourth letter explains how he or she usually carries on his or her public life. If the person is an extravert, the fourth letter points to the dominant function. If the person is an introvert, the fourth letter points to the auxiliary function. The introvert ordinarily keeps the dominant function out of public view.

Test yourself—identify the dominant function in these four personality types. If you're not sure how to do it, refer to "Two Ways to Find Out Your Dominant Function," page 43:

ENFP   INFP   ESTJ   ISTJ

ENFPs enjoy a perceiving life style. They show the world their perceiving function: intuition (N). Intuition is also their dominant function.

INFPs, like ENFPs, run their outer lives by their perceiving function: intuition (N). Unlike ENFPs, however, they do not make intuition their dominant function. Feeling (F) is dominant, and they keep it safely inside where they can protect it.

ESTJs prefer a judging life style. They show the world their judging function: thinking (T). Thinking is also their dominant function.

ISTJs, like ESTJs, run their outer lives by their judging function: thinking (T). Unlike ESTJs, however, they do not make thinking their dominant function. Sensing (S) is dominant, and they keep it safely inside where they can protect it.

If you're sick of functions and letters, just remember these important facts:

If it's important to extraverts, they will quickly show it.

If it's important to introverts, they will often hide it, at least until they feel sure it will be treated with respect.

Introverts would be a real challenge to live with if

it weren't for one redeeming characteristic: when introverts feel at home, they often let down their guard. Instead of fluffing their quills, they may roll over and show
their soft underbellies. But that takes a lot of trust on
their part.

If you want to achieve intimacy with an introvert,
you need to understand his or her nature. Why is the
most cherished function kept inside? To keep it from
being trampled on, rejected, laughed at, cheapened. Introverts will bring out hidden treasures only when they
are good and ready, only when they feel sure that they
will be accepted.

Getting to Know an Introvert

An introverted child with a passion for raising
hamsters is likely to be surprisingly well informed about
the hobby. Hamster genetics, gestation periods, mating
season, litter size, weaning age—the child will know all
these facts and more. Because this child is confident about
his or her knowledge, he or she will readily talk with
others who show interest in hamsters. In fact, a child
who usually has trouble saying a complete sentence may
begin spilling out paragraphs and even chapters. Interest
and knowledge give the introvert courage to open up.

An introverted child who is with someone he or she
completely trusts is not afraid of rejection or ridicule.
This child also feels free to open up. Precious innermost
thoughts can be shared because they will be valued. Confidences that would never be revealed outside the family
circle will be freely exchanged within it—so long as the
introvert's trust is never violated.

If you love an introvert and want to get to know
him or her better, keep these ideas in mind:

• Never forget that the world rarely sees what is
truly important to an introvert. Assume that the introvert
has a rich inner life about which you know little.

• Never try to bully your way into an introvert's inner

sanctum. This will force him or her to keep his or her real self even further out of sight.

• Do not expect consistency from an introvert. If he or she is usually orderly, welcome the occasional flash of spontaneity. If he or she tends to be compliant, be thankful for the rare show of firmness. These are hints of the treasured inner life.

• Show interest in the introvert's interests. Encourage him or her to talk about hobbies, goals, passions, ideals. Be prepared to sit back and listen . . . and listen . . . and listen.

• Do not rush an introvert. One of the most noticeable characteristics of introverts is their habit of pausing before they speak or act. They cannot proceed until they get their bearings. Allow your introverted loved one all the time he or she needs as you walk with him or her through the private world.

• Treat an introvert's confidences as a sacred trust. If he or she is willing to give you a treasure from the inner temple, do not profane it by showing it to people who have not earned the introvert's trust; do not diminish it through ridicule, shock, or argument.

An introverted child—or spouse—can be a delightful companion. Introverts' interests and knowledge run deep. Not for them the shallow summer pools across which dragonflies skim. Their minds are more like deep, still wells at the bottom of which lie gold coins and precious stones.

Introverts need extraverts to give them breadth and sunlight. Extraverts need introverts to give them depth and stillness. It may require a great deal of patient study before an introvert and an extravert understand each other, but the resulting balance and harmony make the effort well worthwhile.

CHAPTER 5

Finding Your Child's Type

BY now you have decided upon your own type, studied the differences that show up in people of different personality traits, learned how the characteristics work together, and discovered your favorite function. You know a lot about personality type theory—but how do you apply this to your children?

Very, very carefully.

Jung was persuaded that a person's personality type is inborn. If a person is born an introvert, he will never become an extravert, even though he may learn to enjoy social situations. If a person is born an intuitive type, she will never turn into a sensing type, even though she may develop her powers of observation.

That, however, does not mean that a person's personality type will be obvious from birth. Some children will give evidence of some of their preferences before they are out of diapers, but many others will be hard to identify until they are in junior high or even later.

Don't Label Your Children

Even if you are quite sure you know your child's personality type, don't put a label on him or her. A label may help me choose the right can of food; it may help me avoid costly mistakes in cleaning a garment; it may even tell me something about the quality or at least snob appeal of something I want to buy. Labels are appropriate for things; they are inappropriate and dangerous for people.

In many ancient religions a name was extremely powerful. Children were given descriptive or prophetic names. *Jacob*, for example, means "he grasps the heel" because that is what he did to his twin brother, Esau, at birth. His name foreshadowed his theft of Esau's birthright and blessing (Genesis 27:36).

Saying the name, in some religions, became the key to gaining power over the person. That may be why the Egyptian-trained Moses asked for God's name at the burning bush, and it is probably why God had Adam name all the animals—to show the authority delegated to human beings. It is why the Israelites would never pronounce the name of their God. It is also why "naming the demon" is part of exorcism.

In today's first-name society the ancient belief about names is all but forgotten. Some of us, however, replace names with psychological labels. Even if we would not label our children "neurotic," "schizophrenic," or "passive-aggressive," we might be tempted to call them ESFPs or INTJs.

If I label my daughter an introvert, I may begin to neglect her outgoing side. If I label her a feeling type, I may not notice when she does a superb job of analysis. If I label my son a sensing type, I may be baffled by his occasional wild bursts of imagination. If I say he is perceiving, I may write off the times he is decisive.

It is particularly dangerous when *parents* label children. We have a sometimes terrifyingly large influence

Four Steps to Take When
Guessing Somebody Else's Type

Whenever you guess somebody else's type, especially somebody too young to identify his or her own preferences, you can never be absolutely sure that your guess is correct. Proceed with extreme caution! The individual is always the last word about his or her own personality type, because type is based on *preferences*, not skills. You may be able to tell me I don't intuit very well, but you can't tell me I don't prefer intuition over sensing. You may notice that I use logic skillfully, but you can't infer that I prefer thinking over feeling.

Still, you can learn valuable information about your children if you employ the scientific method you learned in ninth-grade biology:

1. Observe your child.
2. Form a hypothesis (guess your child's type).
3. Test the hypothesis (relate to your child as if he or she preferred that type).
4. Discard the hypothesis if it doesn't work and start over.

Never, never try to mold a person to fit a type. Instead, use type to understand and appreciate the marvelous variety of people God created and to help your own little people grow up to be all he meant them to be.

on our little people. If we expect them to behave in a certain way, they often do (or at certain ages they do just the opposite—but that too is reacting to parental expectation).

A parent who decides a three-year-old child is an INTP has decided too much. Three-year-olds have barely begun to develop their ways of perceiving and judging. Their inner and outer lives both are still extremely restricted. If the parent really wants the child to grow up to be an INTP, the child may try very hard to do so. Or in frustration, the child may mold himself or herself into an ESFJ just to get even. Neither result is good—unless the child really is an INTP or an ESFJ. Jung observed what may happen to children whose parents pressure them to develop a particular personality pattern:

When the mother's own attitude is extreme, a similar attitude can be forced on the children too, thus violating their individual disposition, which might have opted for another type if no abnormal external influences had intervened. As a rule, whenever such a falsification of type takes place as a result of parental influence, the individual becomes neurotic later, and can be cured only by developing the attitude consonant with his nature.[1]

Let Your Children Tell You Their Types

Does that mean it's time to close this book and forget about personality types? Not at all. In time your children will be old enough to identify their own personality types, or at least certain characteristics.

At age fifteen one of my daughters was not sure if she preferred sensing or intuition, but she knew beyond a shadow of a doubt that she was introverted, thinking, and judging. At the same age my other daughter was not sure if she was introverted or extraverted, but she was fiercely proud of being intuitive, feeling, and perceiving.

Even though I have been observing these girls for their whole lives, I could easily mistake Molly for an extravert. Her insistence that she is not—"Mom, what you see is only acting"—gives me important information about how she wants to be treated.

Likewise, at times I could mistake Heidi for a thinking type. But when I raise the possibility with her, she is offended. She *values* being a feeling type—and this also gives me important information about how to relate to her.

I do not label my daughters, but I allow them to give me information about themselves. This in turn helps me relate to them in ways that are meaningful to them.

But what about dealing with small children who are too young to understand type theory? Here again it is important to let the children give you information. The difference is that you will gain this information by watching them and listening to them, not by testing them or discussing type theory with them.

Perceive More Often Than You Judge

To let our children tell us their types, we need to use perceiving more than judging.

Whether we are sensing or intuitive types, it is important to use our senses. Our eyes tell us what our children are doing; our ears let us know what they are saying; our sense of touch warns us that they need an extra blanket or are running fevers.

It is also important to use our intuition. What could this action, that statement, possibly mean? Where can this behavior, that preference take the child in five years? What does this child most need from me, the parent?

It is usually best to use our judging functions with our children only when absolutely necessary, and to realize that the older the children, the less necessary it should be. Judging functions say, "This is what you ought to do." Thinking judgment adds, "because it is clearly true, logical, and correct." Feeling judgment adds, "because it is certainly right, good, and considerate."

Obviously parents must instruct their children, and both thinking and feeling are important in that task. But if parents insist on instructing them in every tiny detail of running their lives, many children will break down under an "ought" overload. The situation is even worse if parents insist they know the way the children ought to *be*.

A thinking-judging parent may believe that all good children are organized, efficient, and decisive. A feeling-perceiving parent may believe that all good children are warm, enthusiastic, and imaginative. If these parents try to mold their children into pre-ordained personality types, they may find themselves up against a brick wall.

Far better for the parents to turn down the volume

on their judging function, turn it up on their perceiving function, and listen to what the kids are telling them.

One way to sharpen your perceiving is to ask your child questions:

• Do you enjoy playing by yourself? Or would you rather play with friends?

• What did you notice about that restaurant? (Is your child's answer a detailed description of the place, a critical analysis of the service, a comment about the server's personality? Or does your child say, "I'm sorry, but I was thinking about something else and didn't notice anything?")

• Why do you want to do that? (Does your child give logic, truth, popular opinion, or moral values as motivation?)

Another way to perceive more clearly is to make suggestions and see how they are received. "You could invite Robbie over to play." "Tell me what you think heaven will be like." "Think about how that made her feel." "Let's just go and see what happens." Are your suggestions met with enthusiasm? Resistance? Dutiful compliance?

Look At Individual Transactions

It is less important to know if a child is, say, an introvert or an extravert than to know what the child is doing at a given moment. Is the child in her bedroom reading? She is introverting. Is she rounding up the neighbor kids for a game of tag? She is extraverting. Is he following you around demanding explanations ("Why does the sun set?" "Why do dogs have tails?")? He is extraverting. Is he looking up answers to his questions in the encyclopedia? He is introverting.

Obviously, a normal child does a lot of introverting and a lot of extraverting every day.

Similarly, it is less important to know if a child is a thinking type or a feeling type than to see how the child is handling a given decision. Is she making lists of reasons for and against? She is using thinking judgment. Is he wondering how Mom, Dad, Uncle Harry, and the dog will react to his choice? He is using feeling judgment.

Every normal child bases some decisions on thinking, some on feeling, just as he or she sometimes senses and sometimes intuits, sometimes judges and sometimes perceives.

Rather than labeling little Larry an ESTJ, you might observe that today he (1) played with friends from 9:00 A.M. until the sun went down, (2) spent most of the day building an intricate road system for the group's trucks and cars, (3) insisted that his portion of the transportation network be laid out in parallel one-way streets, and (4) persuaded most of the other children to follow his plan.

Indeed, today Larry acted very much like an ESTJ and probably wished to be treated as such—but allow him the freedom to act like an INFP tomorrow, if he so chooses. Remember that childhood is a magical time when people can try on any identity they please. Someday they will find the one that best fits, but if we try to rush them into it, we risk making Procrustes' mistake: Rather than adapting his beds to fit his captives, he stretched or shortened his captives to fit his beds.

Use a Personality Type Inventory

As long as you let your children tell you their types, try to perceive more than you judge, look at individual transactions, and refuse to label your children, it's safe for you to use a personality type inventory to help you understand them better.

If the children are twelve or older, arrange for them to take the MBTI, or ask them to take the Word Choice Quiz in this book. (An exceptionally good reader might be able to do this at nine or ten.)

If they are in primary school, you may be able to arrange for them to take the Murphy-Meisgeier Type

Indicator for Children (MMTIC), designed specifically for use by teachers. See the bibliography for addresses of MMTIC distributors.

If your children take a type indicator, be sure they get a good explanation of what their letters mean. If the person who gives the indicator does not do this in a way your children can understand, do it yourself. Without an explanation, the children will have no way to agree or disagree with the results—and even though the MBTI and the MMTIC are excellent instruments, they are not infallible.

If your children are younger or if you do not want them to take a type indicator, simply observe them. What do you see?

1. Does your child . . .

_____ act quickly, sometimes without thinking?

_____ get tired of long, slow jobs or games?

_____ enjoy learning by doing?

_____ chatter?

_____ enjoy new activities?

_____ have many friends?

_____ want to do things with others?

_____ care what other children think?

_____ unload emotions as they occur?

These are all characteristics of extraverts. Thus when your child does these things, he or she **is** extraverting.

2. Does your child . . .

_____ think before acting?

_____ work or play patiently for long periods of time?

_____ enjoy learning by reading?

_____ keep things to himself or herself?

_____ hesitate to try something new?

_____ have a few close friends?

_____ want a quiet space to work or play in?

_____ set his or her own standards despite others' opinions?

_____ bottle up emotions?

These are all characteristics of introverts. Thus when your child does these things, he or she is introverting.

3. Does your child . . .

_____ enjoy familiar activities and routine?
_____ want to know the right way to do things?
_____ observe carefully and remember lots of details?
_____ memorize easily?
_____ ask, "Did it really happen?"
_____ like coloring books?
_____ enjoy collecting things?
_____ enjoy working with his or her hands?
_____ seem steady and patient?

These are all characteristics of sensing types. Thus when your child does these things, he or she is perceiving through the senses.

4. Does your child . . .

_____ enjoy learning new things?
_____ enjoy being different?
_____ learn quickly but forget details?
_____ have a vivid imagination?
_____ enjoy imaginative stories?
_____ use toys in new and original ways?
_____ often lose things?
_____ quickly go from one new interest to another?
_____ work and play in fits and starts?

These are all characteristics of intuitive types. Thus when your child does these things, he or she is perceiving through the intuition.

5. Does your child . . .

_____ ask "Why?" a lot?
_____ insist on logical explanations?
_____ get alarmed if someone is treated unfairly?
_____ like to arrange things in orderly patterns?
_____ show more interest in ideas than in people?
_____ hold firmly to his or her beliefs?
_____ seem uncomfortable with affection?

_____ want rules in games established and kept?
_____ like to be praised for doing something
           competently?

These are all characteristics of thinking types. Thus when your child does these things, he or she is making thinking judgments.

6. Does your child . . .

_____ like to talk or read about people?
_____ want to be praised for caring for others?
_____ get alarmed if someone is unhappy?
_____ tell stories expressively, in great detail?
_____ try to be tactful, even if that means lying?
_____ show more interest in people than in ideas?
_____ generally agree with his or her friends' opinions?
_____ want to be told you love him or her?
_____ relate well to other children, teachers, relatives?

These are all characteristics of feeling types. Thus when your child does these things, he or she is making feeling judgments.

7. Does your child . . .

_____ like to know what is going to happen?
_____ know how things "ought to be"?
_____ enjoy making choices?
_____ usually work before playing?
_____ discipline himself or herself?
_____ have definite goals?
_____ have strong opinions?
_____ keep a well-ordered room?
_____ want to be in charge?

These are all characteristics of judging types. Thus when your child does these things, he or she is relating to the world through his or her judging function.

8. Does your child . . .

_____ enjoy spontaneity?
_____ show a lot of curiosity?
_____ enjoy sampling new experiences and ideas?

_____ turn work into play?
_____ overextend himself or herself?
_____ adapt well to changing circumstances?
_____ keep an open mind?
_____ not object to having things out of place?
_____ want to understand whatever's happening?

These are all characteristics of perceiving types. Thus when your child does these things, he or she is relating to the world through his or her perceiving function.

Always Be Open to Changing Your Perception

Of the characteristics evaluated by the MBTI, the easiest to see in children is usually extraversion/introversion. This may be evident when a child is only a few months old.

Often the other characteristics develop later. It requires a certain command of language, thought processes, and the five senses to become adept in sensing or intuiting. This difference may show up as early as age two or three or it may not be clear until the child is in school.

When Murphy and Meisgeier developed their type indicator for children, they discovered that the majority of children—even boys—show a strong preference for feeling over thinking. Eighty percent of the girls they tested and two-thirds of the boys chose feeling; yet in the adult population only about sixty percent of the women and forty percent of the men do. Apparently the thinking preference develops later in some people.

It is sometimes hard to identify whether a child prefers interacting with the world through judging or perceiving. Properly understood, both judging and perceiving can be virtues. But sometimes parents think that the absence of well-developed judgment means the child prefers perceiving. This is not necessarily true. Self-discipline, decisiveness, managerial ability may be evident in a young child—or may not be developed until a person is in his or her twenties. If a child who seems weak in these areas also seems strong in adaptability, curiosity, and spontaneity, the child probably prefers perceiving. If no definite preferences appear, it's just too early to call the vote.

Once again, *don't label your children.* Or if you simply can't resist labeling them, keep an assortment of labels handy—sixteen of them. Label your children one way today, another way tomorrow, a third way when appropriate. Use the whole pile of labels to help you understand them and nurture them however they need to be nurtured today, right now.

When children are young, only one thing is absolutely certain about them—they are changing and growing. Quicker than we parents can believe.

1. C. G. Jung, *Psychological Types* (Princeton, N.J.: Princeton University Press, 1971), p. 332.

PART 2

CHAPTER 6

Find a Comfortable Parenting Style

My friend Ann is a very busy woman with two school-aged children, a more-than-full-time job, and a husband who is on the road a great deal. In spite of the continual challenge of juggling her schedule, however, she says she is much happier now than she was five years ago when she was a full-time homemaker.

"That was a much more frustrating time," she told me. "I never felt I had anything to show for my work at the end of the day. I could never say, 'There, that's finished. I did that.' I seemed to have no accomplishments."

Ann is a dedicated mother who does not downplay the importance of spending those years with her children. She knows that laying a foundation of security and trust in a young child's life is a major accomplishment. But the repetitive work of the full-time homemaker is difficult for her to enjoy.

I was interested in Ann's reaction to staying home because my experience was quite different. For me the best part about staying home with small children was being freed from the need to set goals and achieve them. As I saw it, my primary reason for being home was so that I could respond to the children's needs as they occurred. I never minded putting off ironing so that the girls and I could read another chapter in *The Chronicles of Narnia;* I was always happy to leave my typewriter in order to watch the hamsters mate.

This is not to say that being a full-time mother to young children was easy for me. It was not. Several times I perched precariously close to the edge of depression. My problem was not lack of accomplishment—it was loneliness.

During the eight years between our first daughter's birth and our second daughter's first day of school, we lived in six apartments or houses in three different states. Every year or two I had to start making new friends, and that was not easy when I spent my days with two small children and no car in a suburban house. I hurt, and I didn't know why.

If Ann and I had known about personality types in those days of full-time child rearing, we might have understood our predicaments.

Two Moms, Two Styles

Ann is an INTJ. It is important to her to be able to plan, predict, and schedule. She likes to have control of her environment. Full of wonderful ideas, she enjoys working them out in reality. To do this, she needs large blocks of undisturbed time for concentrated study and effort.

I am an ENFP. I like spontaneous excursions, the intrusion of the unexpected, a certain amount of chaos. I'm happiest when living near friends who frequently drop in unannounced. I like working with them on projects we both enjoy; I like tossing ideas back and forth with them; I like packing up their kids and mine and going places together.

Four Groups of Types

David Keirsey, a clinical psychologist from California who has spent many years studying personality type theory, arranges the sixteen types revealed by the MBTI into four distinctive groups. Each group contains four MBTI types that share two particular letters. These groups, called *temperaments*, are a handy way of talking about some of the practical aspects of personality differences.

The SJ temperament (ESTJ, ESFJ, ISTJ, ISFJ) wants duty, order, responsibility, usefulness. SJs respect law and order and uphold tradition, and they are often attracted to professions in business.

The SP temperament (ESTP, ESFP, ISTP, ISFP) wants action, freedom, spontaneity, variety. SPs look for joy in the experience of the moment, and they are often attracted to the visual or performing arts.

The NT temperament (ENTJ, ENTP, INTJ, INTP) wants competence, control, perfection, understanding. NTs look for logic and coherence in their living and in their thinking, and they are often attracted to the sciences.

The NF temperament (ENFJ, ENFP, INFJ, INFP) wants meaning, authenticity, inspiration, communication. NFs long for unity of purpose and spirit among human beings, and they are often attracted to the liberal arts.

Both Ann and I are good mothers who love our children and spend an enormous amount of time and energy caring for them. Our devotion to our families is not in question. Because of our different needs and desires, however, our reactions to different aspects of child rearing are quite different. The Myers-Briggs Type Indicator helps explain how this works. Look at some possible effects of the preferences measured by the MBTI:

Extraversion/Introversion

Extraverts are drawn to the outer world of events, people, activities, and physical objects. All parents act like extraverts some of the time. They interact with their children; get involved in community or school activities;

initiate excursions, adventures, and vacations.

Introverts, by contrast, are drawn to the inner world where ideas are born, sense impressions registered and enjoyed, problems worked out, and emotions savored. All parents act like introverts some of the time. They find a quiet early morning place to read Scripture and pray; lock the bathroom door and enjoy a magazine for a few moments; sink blissfully into the silence of the 2 A.M. feeding; share deep concerns and joys as they tuck a nearly grown child into bed.

Parents who prefer extraversion may feel comfortable with small children's incessant demands. They may enjoy interruptions and be amused by chatterboxes. They tend not to be overwhelmed by large groups of children, and their homes may sometimes look like the neighborhood youth center. On the other hand, extraverts may feel trapped and desperate if child care consistently isolates them from other adults or if it regularly keeps them from pursuing their own interests.

Parents who prefer introversion may actually enjoy the isolation of providing full-time child care, especially if the kids take naps or play happily outdoors for hours at a time and leave the parents free to pursue their individual interests. Introverted parents may also enjoy forming intense, one-on-one relationships with their children. This may take the form of teaching them, enjoying hobbies or sports with them, or talking about values and feelings. Introverts, however, may feel overwhelmed by the unending extraversion that parenting often demands, especially if their children are extraverts.

Sensing/Intuition

Sensing means taking in information through the five senses and paying close attention to it. All parents use their sensing part of the time. In fact, many parents notice that the arrival of a new baby improves their sensing ability remarkably. Parents who once could sleep through a three-alarm fire now leap out of bed for a tiny whimper. Parents who once refused to take their eyes off the TV screen now seem to be able to see what their children are doing directly behind them. And what new parent has not delighted in a baby's velvety softness, chuckles and gurgles, wide trusting eyes, and even unaccustomed smells?

Intuiting means taking in information through the senses but jumping immediately into new ways of interpreting, combining, and using this information. All parents use their intuition part of the time. Intuition may suggest when a child needs encouragement or special help. It may help the parents come up with better ways to house, clothe, and educate the children. It may help them make decisions by keeping them alert to all the possible consequences.

Both sensing and intuition are ways of perceiving the world, and both are vital to good parenting. Parents need to be keenly aware of both facts (a yellow pencil is lying on the floor near the electrical outlet) and possibilities ("Oh goody—a new shape-sorting toy!"). In fact, keeping up with all the sensing and intuiting required of parents can seem like a full-time job.

Parents who prefer sensing may be exhausted by their children's headlong rush from one stage to the next, by the constant need to look behind the facts to the interpretation and to devise new strategies for new situations.

Parents who prefer intuition may be worn out by the eternal vigilance they must maintain, keeping track not only of the children's everyday needs but also of their whereabouts and activities every moment.

So whether you prefer sensing or intuition, you're likely to be somewhat drained by parenting—that's the name of the game. When I was fifteen, I noticed that my mother seemed extremely tired much of the time. I didn't know if her job was too much for her or if her health was declining, but I knew something was amiss.

When I was twenty-one I suddenly realized that Mother no longer seemed exhausted. Her job and health had not changed. The only major change in her life was that for over a year she had had no children at home. Could a model child like me have worn out her mother? You bet.

Thinking/Feeling

Thinking means making decisions objectively, basing them on firm principles and logical consequences. All parents use their thinking some of the time. "If you touch that pan, you will burn your finger" is a thinking type of statement. When parents analyze and organize, they are using their thinking judgment.

Feeling means making decisions subjectively, basing them on strongly held values and personal identification with an individual or situation. All parents use their feeling some of the time. "How would you feel if your sister did that to you?" is a question that shows concern for feeling-type values. When parents sympathize and try to create harmony, they are using their feeling judgment.

Parents who prefer using thinking judgment often are good disciplinarians. They are likely to use logical consequences as often as possible, making the punishment fit the crime. These parents enjoy being reasonable, and so they may find it hard to know how to relate to children who, for one reason or another, are not relating reasonably to them. That's why they may feel like taking six months in Antarctica when their children turn two or hit puberty.

A great many leaders in business and industry, by the way, combine thinking and judging. One study found that executive women were more likely to prefer extraversion and thinking than non-executive women. Thus parents who prefer thinking, especially if they also prefer extraversion and judging, may have a strong career orientation. For some thinking types, work outside the home may be a psychological necessity. Fortunately, such parents tend to be well organized and strongly disciplined.

Parents who prefer using feeling judgment are often emotionally close to their children. They often understand how the children are feeling, and they tend to know how to comfort, calm, and inspire them. These parents may be tempted to apply discipline inconsistently, however, and their children may learn to manipulate them. Because feeling-type parents want to make their children happy, they may often feel guilty.

Judging/Perceiving

Parents who prefer to interact with the world through *judging* like to plan ahead and make decisions. All parents use judging some of the time. They make schedules, establish household rules, say yes or no to the kids' requests.

Parents who prefer to interact with the world through *perceiving* like to leave things open for as long as possible, adapting to whatever comes up. All parents use perceiving some of the time. They change their work plans when kids get sick, sit down and really listen when a child needs comfort or advice, scrap their schedules and go to the beach because it's September and the sun is shining.

Parents who prefer judging are likely to have well-ordered homes. Meals are served on time; washed and ironed clothing is always available; and children never miss field trips because their parents forgot to return the permission slip. On the other hand, these parents may experience frustration if their children do not wish to follow schedules or fit in with the household system that the parents have so thoughtfully designed.

Parents who prefer perceiving are likely to be available when the children need them. They rarely say no before thoughtfully considering the child's request, and they are often willing to change their plans if a child has a better idea. Nevertheless, these parents may make promises they forget to fulfill or show up late for important dates with the kids. They may experience frustration over the planning and scheduling necessary for the smooth operation of a home.

Putting Similar Types Together

Looking at the four pairs of characteristics, one pair at a time, explains a great deal about why one parent reacts to her kids one way while another reacts to his a completely different way. It doesn't tell the whole story, however.

A personality type (such as INFJ or ESTP) is more than the sum of the characteristics represented by each letter. The characteristics interrelate to produce patterns and trends that could not be inferred from any one characteristic taken alone. Certain combinations of characteristics may lead to one style of parenting, while other combinations may lead to another.

A helpful way to think about the interrelation of personality characteristics is proposed by David Keirsey in his book *Please Understand Me* (see "Four Groups of Types," page 67). Keirsey, a clinical psychologist, speaks of four *temperaments* (groups of personality types with many traits in common): SJ, SP, NT, and NF. An SJ, for example, is any person whose personality type code contains both an S and a J. From now on when I say *type* I will mean one of the sixteen MBTI personality types. When I say *temperament* I'll be talking about one of Keirsey's four groups. For your convenience, both words are in the glossary.

It is not hard to see how Keirsey's four temperaments relate to parenting styles. They go a long way toward explaining, for example, why some women enjoy staying home full time with their children and why others are happier combining career and motherhood. Look at these characteristics of the four temperaments:

SJs, conservative at heart, are most likely to want a

traditional family structure: Dad working outside the home, Mom working in it, several children, pets, a station wagon, and regular church commitments. It is hard to keep SJs from doing their duty; they simply would not feel right if they didn't. An SJ mother may feel isolated and unappreciated, but if she believes she should stay home with her children, she will stay there unless financial pressure forces her into the workplace. When an SJ mother has to work, she turns her work as well as her home into a duty and usually does a good job in both areas. She may, however, suffer from guilt and fatigue.

Blanche, my own SJ mother, believed that a mother's place is with her children. She wanted to earn enough extra money, however, to send me to Christian schools. Typical of a sensing type, she found a down-to-earth solution: part-time secretarial work during my school hours. Typical of a judging type, once she made her decision she carried it out efficiently. Her employers loved her attention to detail and her sense of responsibility; I loved the warm house and fresh cookies that greeted me when I came home. My mother was not driven by career goals or idealism. She knew her duty and she did it—happily and well.

NTs, concerned for competence, are likely to want to invest themselves in their careers. Achievement is usually important to them, and they often plan carefully so that they can use their skills and raise children at the same time. If an NT mother stops using her skills and training in order to devote full time to her children, she risks becoming critical and overbearing. She may make her children her career, expecting them to behave in a way that will prove her competence as a mother.

Elisabeth, an NT friend, spent fifteen years climbing the career ladder before she married and had two children. "My career is very important to me," she told me, "and I don't dare drop out for six or eight years." Elisabeth has taken advantage of the computer revolution by setting up an independent business with headquarters in her home. She has chosen not to work full time while her children are preschoolers, but two days a week they go to the sitter and she goes to her upstairs office. Elisabeth enjoys motherhood—and she also enjoys the professional recognition that she continues to earn.

SPs, more interested in process than outcome, may be just as career oriented as NTs. Experience rather than achievement is important to SPs, and they need to make time for the art, craft, sport, or skill that captivates them. If an SP mother ignores this important part of her personality, she risks either becoming depressed or giving up her home responsibilities altogether. Fortunately, many things that delight her are likely to delight her children also. Rather than giving up her interests, she can share them. (Joke: How does an SP call the kids to dinner? "Hey, everybody, get in the car!")

Winnie, an SP colleague, still laughs about the time the campus police picked up her then-four-year-old daughter. "They thought she was lost. Actually she was on her way to my office and knew exactly where she was going. She enjoyed the ice cream they gave her, though."

A woman with an immense capacity for enjoyment, Winnie gives all four of her children the freedom she requires for herself. This does not mean she leaves them unsupervised. Between herself, her husband, and her mother, the children are well trained and well watched. They are expected, however, to know how to take care of themselves—and they do. This allows Winnie to teach classes, entertain friends, and still have time to do things with her family. Her home is always full of people, activity, and laughter.

NFs, craving significance, want their work to make a difference for the human race. They also want to be appreciated. This creates a dilemma for an NF mother. If she is surrounded by people who believe that nurturing children and spouses is the most important task a person can do, she may feel good about staying home with her family (although her nurturing style is likely to be a bit eccentric when compared to that of the SJ mother). If, by contrast, she regularly hears motherhood debased and downgraded, she may have a hard time feeling that her daily tasks are meaningful, even if deep down she believes they are.

Margaret, an NF relative, refused to hold a full-time job until her children were almost out of high school and the prospect of college tuition bills began to terrify her. For Margaret, caring for a family is the most meaningful job in the world. She has turned it into a cause: she has taught natural childbirth and breastfeeding classes, counseled distraught couples, and welcomed the lonely into her home. Margaret sometimes feels uneasy because she feels that popular opinion is on the side of the working woman, but she usually allows her idealism to override her doubts.

Not a One-Way Street

Four temperaments, four women, four approaches to motherhood. Each of the four women is a conscientious mother, because each has approached motherhood in the style best suited to her temperament. Blanche may not know why Margaret needs to have a cause, and Elisabeth might think Winnie's laissez-faire attitude is a sure route to disaster, but that's okay. The four women are happy, and their ten children are thriving.

God created us with different personalities and different needs so that we could accomplish different tasks as members of Christ's body. Being a parent is probably the most important assignment most of us will ever be given. But that doesn't mean all parents should adopt the same approach any more than all executives, physicians, or pastors should be carbon copies of one another. Some will be orderly, some casual. Some will plan, and some will improvise. Some, like my friend Ann, will want and need a major career commitment in addition to home duties. Others, like me, will combine part-time work with part-time homemaking. Still others, including some fathers, will make their best contribution if they are home full time. In fact, the very worst advice anyone could give a conscientious parent would be to adopt someone else's approach.

Children have certain basic requirements: food, shelter, supervision, and clothing; a sense of security, the experience of being loved, and opportunities to develop. Different parents meet those requirements in different ways—even within the same family. Rather than trying to be model parents after someone else's pattern, mothers and fathers should discover their own preferences, their own skills, their own gifts.

And if a husband and wife learn that their styles are not quite compatible, they should rejoice! Their differences can give them one more chance to stretch and grow, as we will see in the next chapter.

CHAPTER 7

Strengthen Your Marriage

THIS is a book about parents and children, not about husbands and wives. But each child has two parents, and if those parents live together and love each other, the child has many big advantages:

- twice as much loving
- two styles of discipline
- two models of adult behavior
- daily lessons in communication
- preparation for lasting relationships

I agree with the sage who observed, "The best thing a man can do for his children is to love their mother." Obviously the converse is also true: the best thing a woman can do for her children is to love their father. For normal, healthy development, children need strong parents united in their love for each other. Deprived of this, they—and the parent who raises them—have to work overtime to lay the foundations some other way.

If type theory can help you understand your

children, it can also help you understand your mate. If it gives you insights that strengthen your marriage, your children will be affected. And that is why, when you want to become a better parent, strengthening your marriage is a good place to start.

It's Okay to Be Yourself

One way type theory can improve marriages is by showing the spouses that it's okay to be the way they are. A man who is attracted to a passionate, extravagant ESFP and then tries to change her into a dutiful, thrifty ISTJ may have a problem on his hands—not with the woman, who hasn't changed, but with his expectations, which are clearly unrealistic.

It was a great day for our marriage when I figured out that David's strong work orientation was not a perverse attempt to eliminate fun from our lives. Instead, it was a typical INTJ behavior which could get out of hand, but which he kept well under control. Actually, as I came to realize, David's interest in working benefited us enormously. After all, every family needs at least one person willing to pay the bills—and for him, going to work was fun!

At the same time I realized that my own reluctance to immerse myself in a career also benefited our family. My preferred approach to life made me available to them most of the time, and I did not need to feel guilty about working one project at a time rather than steadily, fifty hours a week. If it was okay for David to act like an INTJ, it was also okay for me to act like an ENFP. Actually, our preferences complemented each other nicely.

Judging both of us by an INTJ standard, I could be considered unfocused. Judging both of us by an ENFP standard, David could be considered driven. However, neither description fits. Judging us by our own standards, David is a conscientious, hard-working man who also cares deeply for his family, and I am a caring wife and

Three Ways to Handle Differences in Marriage

Isabel Briggs Myers, developer of the Myers-Briggs Type Indicator, was an INFP happily married to an ISTJ for over sixty years. Their personality differences, in fact, motivated Mrs. Myers and her mother, Katharine Briggs (INFJ) to begin their lifelong study of psychological type. Here are some words of wisdom Mrs. Myers gave at a conference on the MBTI:

> If there are differences in marriage, there will always come times when a difference in point of view is unresolvable. You have one point of view, and your partner has another, and there you are! Now there are three ways of treating that kind of thing.

> You can consider that it is wrong of your partner to be different from you, and you can be indignant. That diminishes your partner and gets you nowhere.

> Or you can consider that it is wrong of you to be different from your partner and be depressed. That diminishes you and gets you nowhere.

> The proper solution is to consider that the two of you are justifiably and interestingly different, and be amused.[1]

mother who also values professional attainments.

If personality type theory frees husbands and wives to be themselves and to let their partners be themselves also, it makes a major contribution to family happiness. But it does even more than this. Another way type theory can improve marriages is by showing them how people of different types can work together to achieve balance and wholeness.

Do Opposites Attract?

It seems obvious—opposites attract initially, but in marriage they can drive each other crazy.

A number of researchers, suspecting this to be the

case, have investigated couples of similar and of widely differing personality types. Two conclusions seem well established:

First, opposites do not necessarily attract. Married couples are far more likely to be similar in two or three MBTI-measured traits than mere chance would explain.

Second, opposites do not necessarily have trouble living together. Personality type similarity or difference seems to have no statistical effect on marital happiness or discord.

Intuitives and sensing types might have a hard time understanding each other; thinking and feeling types might have trouble arriving at a mutual decision; judging and perceiving types might arrange their lives quite differently—but statistically speaking, none of those differences is likely to make a marriage any weaker, just as similarity in those areas is unlikely to make it any stronger.

Of course, we all have an uptight Aunt Mabel who drove poor old laid-back Uncle Harry to distraction with her demanding ways. But for every Mabel and Harry, it seems, there's a Jabel and Mary who absolutely adore each other because they're so different.

Psychological researcher Ruth Sherman, after an intensive investigation into personality type differences and marital satisfaction, concluded that only one difference has any statistically discernible effect. When the man is introverted and the woman extraverted, a number of misunderstandings and disagreements may occur.

Dr. Sherman explains: "When an introvert lives with an extravert . . . the needs of one are often in direct conflict with the needs of the other, and it is often impossible for both sets of needs to be satisfied at the same time."[2]

Interestingly, when the situation is reversed and an extraverted man has an introverted wife, no particular problems occur. Why, then, should extraverted women and introverted men have trouble getting along? Some possibilities have been suggested:

• Since extraverts are likely to take the lead while introverts step back and ponder, perhaps they feel out of step in a society that expects men to be the chief initiators.

• If the introverted man works in an office all day and the extraverted woman stays home, maybe both of them feel ready to explode by dinnertime. He desperately needs restorative peace and quiet just when she hungers for activity and socialization.

• Men, whether extraverts or introverts, often find it hard to reveal their deep emotions. An introverted man is likely to share especially slowly and cautiously. If his extraverted wife attempts to fill their silences with nonstop talking, he may retreat into his inner castle and pull up the drawbridge. This will make her feel like she is living with a stranger.

Meeting Problems Head-on

These potential problems certainly do not mean that introverted men and extraverted women should not marry. Statistics are useful tools for talking about groups, but they often say little about individuals. My ISFJ father and ESFJ mother have been exceptionally happy together for fifty-five years. Their differences do not drive them apart; they help my parents complement each other. My INTJ husband is still happy with his ENFP wife after twenty years. And many of our solidly married friends are also introverted men with extraverted women.

The secret is to anticipate problems and head them off at the pass.

Is the couple uncomfortable when the wife takes the lead? They might try challenging their discomfort: perhaps it's perfectly appropriate for her to initiate some activities. Or the wife might teach herself to wait a moment before acting. If she gives her husband time to reflect, he may be able to lead out just as effectively as she does.

Does the wife need to socialize just when the husband needs to retreat? She can try giving him time to unwind when he arrives home from work, in hopes that he'll feel like mixing later. Or she can encourage him to stay home and read while she goes out with friends. If this is a perpetual problem, maybe both of them need to change their daily activities so that he can spend his work time alone while she spends hers with people.

Has the introverted husband barricaded himself in his private world? Again the wife needs to train herself to slow down, wait in silence, and listen patiently without interrupting whenever he chooses to speak. It may be unfair to put the burden of luring him out on his wife, but it is probably easier to persuade an extravert to shut up than an introvert to butt in.

All combinations, of course, have potential problems. Two extraverts can easily become so swamped by outside commitments that they forget to take time for themselves and for each other. They risk developing a superficial relationship, one that might not survive a time of crisis when a solid foundation of intimacy is imperative. Two extraverts need to plan regular, inviolable times to sit down, relax, and talk with each other.

Two introverts may also find their deep communication breaking down, but for a different reason. Each waiting for the other to initiate sharing, they may end up making assumptions about what the other thinks and feels. Or they could develop the opposite problem—an intense, shared vision, but little activity in the outer world to bring it about. The remedy for two introverts, of course, depends on the problem. Either they need to make a point of sharing their private feelings, or they need to move from sharing into action.

When an extravert is married to an introvert, it can be hard to arrange mutually satisfying activities, and it can be a challenge to be sure the introvert gets his or her say. Still, this combination holds the possibility of

balance. If the extraverted partner draws the couple into the world of action and socializing while the introverted partner draws them into the world of reflection and understanding, both lives will be enriched.

This principle holds true for all the possible marital combinations: sameness may make for easier understanding, but difference may contribute to balance and richness.

Those Flaky Intuitives

Even so, there's no getting around it: sensing types and intuitive types have a hard time understanding each other. This difference between herself and her husband, in fact, was what led Isabel Briggs Myers to a lifelong study of personality.

Sensing types learn through careful observation and fact gathering. Intuitive types learn through a free association of apparently unrelated ideas. A sensing spouse in a bad mood might say the intuitive partner was spacey. The intuitive might respond that the sensing partner was boring. In better spirits, however, the two of them might laud each other for being full of ideas (intuitive) and down to earth (sensing).

A sensing husband once told me what happens when he takes his intuitive wife to a strange city: "She's enthralled by the high rises and the traffic helicopter and the window washers, and I'm frantically saying, 'Watch *out*—did you see what you almost stepped in?'"

In spite of the confusion the sensing-intuitive difference can cause, it does not seem to affect marital satisfaction. Dr. Sherman found that sensing types tend to be quite well satisfied and intuitive types somewhat dissatisfied no matter what type their partners are.

One reason for this, she suggests, "may be that intuitives experience a higher level of expectation than sensates do. . . . Imagination and idealism can create unrealistic fantasies that no mate could possibly satisfy, and unmet expectations result in disappointment and dissatisfaction."[3]

As the intuitive wife of an intuitive husband (and mother of two intuitive children), I have an alternate theory. Intuitives can have a simply marvelous time together, involved as they always are with new projects, new schemes, new ways of thinking. The trouble is, a lot of us really don't much like the nitty-gritty of home maintenance—detailed record keeping, repetitive household chores with little room for originality, constant vigilance against cracks and flakes and other harbingers of disaster. Put two intuitives in charge of a house, and you have a recipe for chaos. If they do the disagreeable tasks, they may start feeling resentful. If they ignore them, the other partner (or the neighbors) may complain.

The moral of the story? If you're an intuitive married to an intuitive, try not to overload on the mutually disagreeable tasks. If you're married to your opposite, be thankful that your partner likes the very jobs that tire you out. And if you're a sensing type married to a sensing type, you don't need a moral. You're probably already doing well.

Using Differences Constructively

Most personality differences between marriage partners are neutral. They can cause conflict, but they can also contribute to growth and balance. It all depends on what the couple does with them. Personality similarities are also neutral. They can foster understanding, but they can also lead to an unhealthy one-sidedness. Again, the couple's personality types are not so important as their willingness to work together.

The thinking-feeling difference is the only one that seems to be sex-linked. By about a three to two ratio, men prefer making decisions logically, analytically, objectively. By the same ratio, women prefer basing their decisions on their personal values.

Thinking types, whether male or female, are apt to put truth over tactfulness; feeling types of both sexes can be easily hurt. Thus a thinking-feeling combination has the potential for missed communication and wounded feelings. On the other hand, it also has the potential for a delicate balance between strength and gentleness, the cool head and the warm heart.

For handling family finances no combination is better than two thinkers. For providing a warm, affectionate atmosphere, two feelers can't be topped. And if the couple is a matched pair of thinkers or feelers, the family is not likely to go far out of balance. If the partners are both thinkers, the woman will probably see to the family's emotional needs. If they are both feelers, the man will most likely provide the necessary toughness. After all, that's how they've been trained.

It's obvious why some judging types married to perceiving types have problems. A person who wants life planned and orderly, married to a person who thrives on improvisation and surprises, needs a well-developed sense of humor. But that doesn't mean judgers should not marry perceivers.

Two judging types know where they are going and get there on time—but they can be so intent on reaching their goal that they forget to have fun along the way. Two perceiving types can have a great deal of fun together—but their party can't go on forever if the work doesn't get done. Put a judger with a perceiver, and you may hit a balance between work and play.

Thus a difference in judging and perceiving, just as in sensing and intuiting or thinking and feeling, neither makes nor breaks a marriage. Sameness can lead to understanding, or it can reinforce negative ways of relating. Difference can lead to balance, or it can result in hostility and stalemate. Often just knowing what to expect from your partner can turn conflict into understanding.

It is wrong to use personality type as an excuse for your own misbehavior. A perceiving type, for example, should never say, "I can't help missing deadlines—I'm a perceiver." Neither should a judging type say, "I can't help jumping to conclusions—I'm a judger." Perceiving types can and must learn to be responsible, just as judging types can and must learn to collect adequate information.

But it can't hurt in a marriage to use personality type to help you look at your spouse's better side—even if he or she occasionally misbehaves. If he isn't ready on time, you don't need to praise his tardiness, but you might say to yourself, "Even so, he is wonderfully tolerant of me." If she cleans your desk and throws away coupons you were planning to use, you don't need to be grateful for her compulsion to organize your affairs, but you might remind yourself, "All the same, she is marvelously talented at running this household."

Because every personality trait has its good side, just as every combination has its strengths, a husband and wife who want to build a strong, loving marriage will be able to find a way—no matter how alike or how different they are.

1. Myers makes a similar statement in *Gifts Differing* (Palo Alto, Calif.: Consulting Psychologists Press, 1980), p. 135.

2. Ruth Sherman, "Psychological Typology and Satisfaction in Intimate Relationships" (unpublished doctoral dissertation, University of Hawaii, 1982), p. 17.

3. Sherman, p. 126.

CHAPTER 8

Improve Family Communication

IT had been another hard day at work, and David was crawling under the covers in hopes of instant oblivion when I cheerfully said, "David, I have a wonderful idea. Let's adopt a child!"

Ten or twenty years ago, such an ill-timed comment could have triggered an explosion. Panic that I was going to upset our budget, our plans, our household! Rage that I had chosen 11 P.M. to drop the bomb! Exasperation that I could not let a week go by without coming up with another far-fetched scheme!

But this time David was ready for me. After living with the MBTI for nearly a decade, he knew just what it means to be an INTJ husband of an ENFP wife. Calmly he inquired, "Are you proposing that as an introvert, having carefully considered the consequences and arrived at a conclusion? Or are you suggesting it as an extravert, having suddenly experienced inspiration and wanting to open a discussion?"

(I should point out that David is a scholar and an editor, and he really does talk like that—especially when

I have just had a bright idea.)

"I guess I'm suggesting it as an extravert," I said.

"That's a relief," said David. "We'll discuss it tomorrow." And he rolled over and went to sleep.

The Strong Silent Type Meets the Chatterbox

Extraverts and introverts can have trouble communicating, especially if they do not understand that they jump into discussions at different points. They may also be put off by each other's style.

An extraverted mother began to worry about her son, age fifteen. Always rather reserved, he now seemed to want to escape the family entirely. The minute he finished eating dinner, he excused himself from the table and was rarely seen before breakfast the next morning. When spoken to, he answered politely, but he never volunteered information that wasn't asked. He did his best to avoid sitting around and talking with his sisters.

Was he feeling hostile and rebellious? Was he depressed? Was he perhaps on drugs? The mother had no clue until a chance encounter with the MBTI stimulated her thinking.

As it turned out, the boy was completely unaware of the impression his mother was receiving. An INTP in his second year of high school, he suddenly found himself with a lot to think about—his future career, his philosophy of life, and especially his homework, which now included one math course and two science courses. This thinking required solitude, so he took advantage of all the alone time he could find. It never occurred to him that his family would find his behavior alarming.

An introverted pastor who liked to spend hours alone in his study reading and preparing sermons was completely unprepared for his first-born, a highly extraverted little boy. John's constant patter was amusing and articulate, but it also was extremely tiring after, say, twenty minutes nonstop.

Thirty-two Communication Pairs

Dr. Flavil Yeakley of Abilene Christian University believes that communication is easiest among people whose personality type codes have the same central letters (S or N, T or F), most difficult when both central letters differ. Certain pairs have more success or problems than others. This is how it works, according to Dr. Yeakley:

If your type is . . .	You are likely to understand an . . .	You may be confused by an . . .
ESTJ	ISTJ	ENFJ
ESFJ	ISFJ	ENTJ
ESTP	ISTP	ENFP
ESFP	ISFP	ENTP
ENTJ	INTJ	ESJF
ENFJ	INFJ	ESTJ
ENTP	INTP	ESFP
ENFP	INFP	ESTP
ISTJ	ESTJ	INFP
ISFJ	ESFJ	INTP
ISTP	ESTP	INFJ
ISFP	ESFP	INTJ
INTJ	ENTJ	ISFP
INFJ	ENFJ	ISTP
INTP	ENTP	ISFJ
INFP	ENFP	ISTJ

The father hit upon a double solution. First, he suggested that John talk with an imaginary playmate part of the time. One playmate turned out not to be enough; John happily invented Buzz and Washington and played all three roles as needed.

Second, John's father found a gentle way to confront his son directly when enough was enough. He would listen intently for a few minutes. Then he would say, "John, that was very interesting, and I want to hear more about it later. Right now, though, my ears are tired."

John understood that. In fact, once he responded, "That's okay, Dad, my mouth is tired too." He would go off with Buzz and Washington for a while; Dad could rest; and then the cycle would begin again.

Confusion and Hurt

If extraverts and introverts have trouble understanding each other, their problems are minor compared with those faced by sensers and intuiters, thinkers and feelers.

"You know what's in our back yard?" a very young intuiter asked. "A big blue dinosaur. He has wings, and there's fire coming out of his mouth."

"Silly," said his sensing sibling. "Dinosaurs have been extinct for zillions of years. And there isn't any fire, or the grass would be burning."

Sensers want the facts, ma'am, and nothing but the facts. Furthermore, they want them in sequence. They are comfortable when they are on familiar territory, and if you're telling them a story, they want you to begin at the beginning and proceed step by step until the end.

Intuiters, by contrast, may have a reckless disregard for facts. They love talking about new ideas, new possibilities. They are bored by the familiar and impatient with step-by-step presentations.

Sensers and intuiters can baffle each other; thinkers and feelers can hurt each other.

Two teen-age sisters were discussing college plans. The younger girl, a strong feeling type, said, "If you decide to go to Megabucks U., I think I'll go there too. Being near you is important to me."

Her sister, an equally strong thinking type, responded, "That's a dumb thing to say. M. U. doesn't have the program you need. I mean, I'd like to have you near me and all that, but you should choose the university with the best department in your field."

Later the girls' mother had a chance to review the exchange with the Thinker. "Your sister wasn't really saying she plans to go to M. U.," the mother said. "She was saying she loves you. She can't bear the prospect of being separated from you next year."

"Oh, no," said the Thinker. "I hope I didn't hurt her feelings. I'll miss her, too. But I still think it would be dumb of her to go to M. U."

The Four Languages

Most families include people of several different types, and not necessarily types that naturally understand each other. How can family members learn to communicate so that they will be heard, to listen so that they will understand?

There are many steps in the communication process. No message is transmitted from one person to another without these four steps at least:

1. A person wants to send a message.
2. The person sends it.
3. Another person receives the message.
4. That person interprets it.

Obviously a lot of messages get lost along the way. The sender may not state the message exactly as he or she thought it:

> Child: But you said we could go to the zoo today.
> Parent: I said we could go if the weather was nice.
> Child: You didn't say anything about the weather. You *promised.*

Or the receiver may not receive it just as it was sent:

> Parent: Would you turn down that music and listen?
> Teen: Are you talking to me?

Or even more likely, the receiver may not interpret it the way the sender meant it to be understood:

> Child: There's a dragon under my bed.
> Parent: Dragons do not exist.

For good communication to exist, people have to speak and listen in the same language.

In practical terms, what do the "languages" of the four functions sound like?

The sensing language is factual and direct. If you want to get a senser's attention, let him or her know exactly what you're talking about as soon as you open your mouth. If you need to discuss a problem with a sensing child, describe it in concrete terms before analyzing it, expressing feelings about it, or trying to solve it. To persuade a sensing child to do something your way, show the child that your approach makes sense. Back up your request with data. When talking to a sensing person, be factual, be practical, and proceed one step at a time.

If the lawn needs mowing, tell your sensing child why, when, and how: "I'd like you to mow the lawn this afternoon because the grass is four inches long. If it's not mowed today, it will start dying underneath. Then when it is eventually mowed, the lawn will be brown. Since rain is predicted for tonight, it would be good to do it right after school. The lawn mower is in the shed; it should be full of gas."

If a sensing person is talking to you, don't look for hidden messages. Try to hear exactly what the speaker is saying—the details, the facts. Don't interrupt; don't rush the other person. If the sensing person is giving a blow-by-blow account, don't push for the point. Try to enjoy each description or assimilate each fact as the speaker presents it.

The intuitive language is enthusiastic and imaginative. If you want to get an intuitive's attention, point out an interesting possibility. If you need to discuss a problem with an intuitive child, encourage the child to help you find the solution. Don't define the problem too narrowly—why settle for an agreement to mow the lawn this week when the child might be willing to devise an entire system of lawn maintenance for you? And don't overwhelm the intuitive with details; he or she won't remember them anyway.

The intuitive child who cheerfully plans lawn care

for the whole summer may be incredibly hard to persuade to mow the lawn on Wednesday, even if Wednesday was the day he or she chose for the task. That's because intuitives of all ages like planning much better than doing. Try associating the routine task with a future pleasure that is still in the planning stages: "How would you like to earn five dollars toward your trip to Washington?"

If an intuitive person is talking to you, don't assume that the speaker's meaning is contained by the words he or she is using. Look for hidden meanings and symbols. Consider the possibilities that the speaker's words are opening up. Encourage intuitives to share their dreams as well as their everyday experiences. And try not to say, "Get your head out of the clouds." Intuitives often do their best work in the stratosphere.

The thinking language is concise. To get a thinker's attention, state your case clearly and without repetition. If you need to discuss a problem with a thinking child, you probably don't risk hurt feelings—but you do risk disdain if you are unable to present a good case. An abundance of factual data may not impress a thinker, but a tightly knit, logical argument will. Keep your cool, no matter how exasperating the thinker may be: thinkers respect calmness and objectivity.

Before agreeing to mow the lawn, the thinker will want to know why. If you have a reason, make it known: "You're the only one who doesn't have another appointment this afternoon, and the grass must be mowed before it rains. The radio says there's a seventy percent chance of heavy rain tonight." (If you don't have a reason, don't be surprised if the lawn doesn't get mowed.)

If a thinker is talking to you, look for the logic in what he or she says. Find the central idea and try to relate other statements to it. Acknowledge clear reasoning. Insist on adequate evidence.

The feeling language is friendly. To get a feeler's attention, show interest in what he or she is doing. If you need to discuss a problem with a feeling child, lay a groundwork of good will before beginning. Let the child know you value him or her. Then present the problem in terms of the effect it is having on people.

A feeling person may not worry about brown lawns or the hazards of mowing in the rain, but he or she will be concerned for your feelings. Try this: "How nice your room looks since you rearranged the furniture! You know, I'm feeling really overwhelmed today. I have a late meeting and I won't get home from work until almost six o'clock. It's supposed to rain, and I hate driving in storms. And then there's the grass—have you seen how long it is? I'm afraid the neighbors must be embarrassed to share the street with us! Say, would you mind mowing the lawn as soon as you get home from school? You can't imagine how grateful I'd feel if that were all done by the time I got home."

If a feeler is talking to you, be especially alert. The simplest statement may contain values, hopes, messages of affection, fears, insecurities. "Oh, no, I have a pimple!" does not call for a discussion of acne medication, but rather for reassurance that the child still looks good.

Learning a New Language

Dr. Flavil Yeakley concluded after extensive research that we are all likely to connect easily with some personality types and to find very little in common with others. His list of easiest and hardest combinations is on page 89. Even without knowing your best and worst matches, though, it's easy to see that if two people's two middle letters match, they are going to communicate much more easily than if their two middle letters are different. NFs understand other NFs better than they understand NTs, SFs, or—especially—STs.

Whatever the cause, one thing is certain: parents and children often have trouble connecting. "Will you listen when I talk?" hisses the exasperated parent through clenched teeth. "My parents never listen to me!"

the teenager wails into the telephone. No doubt the child and the parents all think they are listening—but the language they are listening in is not the language the others are speaking.

Probably some of the languages of communication seem more natural to you than the others. If you are an ISFJ, for example, you very likely feel more comfortable using sensing and feeling ways of communicating than intuitive and thinking ways.

Being at home with two communication styles gives you some flexibility. You can connect with your ENFJ husband through feeling and with your ESTP daughter through sensing. But what can you do to make contact with your INTP son?

It may require some work. As an ISFJ, you relate to the world primarily through feeling; feeling is the most difficult language in the world for your son to understand. You can speak the sensing language quite comfortably also; but that's not much better for an INTP.

If you have a predicament like that, it's time to begin learning a new language. Your son, especially when he is very young, is still learning to use his preferred way of relating to the world. Asking him to change styles at this point would only confuse him and might even make your communication more difficult. Try approaching him as if you too preferred intuition and thinking. Ask a lot of "what ifs." Keep your messages short and logical.

When it's his turn to talk, don't read feeling overtones into his thinking messages. One thinking-type seven-year-old, asked to write in a guest book, inscribed, "I liked everything except the broccoli." His feeling-type mother was appalled. How rude! How likely to hurt the hosts' feelings! The thinking-type hosts, however, were not at all hurt. Like the child, they valued truth over tact. The mother of a thinking-type child might as well learn to do the same thing.

Where appropriate, tactfully help your little intuitive thinker learn a few sensing or feeling skills. "How many animals can you find in this picture?" "How do you suppose she felt when you said that?" But don't expect him to initiate sensing or feeling styles of communication until he's much, much older—if then.

A Practical Hint

We must not leave this discussion of communication without looking at a problem parents face every day. It seems to be in our job description that we are constantly giving directions. "Eat this." "Go there." "Do that." "Watch out!" Most of us give more commands than necessary (and if you doubt that, ask your children for their opinion). A lot of the directions we give are ignored. How can parents use personality type to help them get their directions across?

It's important to realize that children of different types and temperaments respond to directions quite differently. If you give directions according to your personality, not your children's, you can be sure that your directions will be at best only partially followed.

If your child favors both sensing and judging, give detailed directions, one step at a time, in order. Aim to skip nothing, no matter how trivial. When you have finished, go through the entire list again. Better yet, ask your child to repeat it back to you.

To get an intuitive-plus-thinking child to follow your plan, do *not* give SJ-style directions. Give this child directions only once. Outline the major steps, but leave the smaller, more evident steps to the child's imagination. If you give intuitive thinkers more directions than they want, they will tune you out.

An intuitive-plus-feeling child also prefers a broad outline rather than a complete set of directions. This child may daydream through part of your oral presentation, however. To be on the safe side, hand your intuitive feeler a written list of instructions after you have told him or her what you want done—or post it on the refrigerator, where it is unlikely to get lost.

If your child combines sensing with perceiving, spare yourself the effort of giving detailed, clear, or even written directions. These children don't usually like directions. They prefer to figure things out for themselves. Point your sensing-plus-perceiving child the way you want him or her to go, and hope the internal compass is working.

Effective communication is a skill that can be learned. Businesses all over the country are teaching their employees how to give and receive messages according to the types and temperaments of the people they want to reach. And if communication is important to people who see each other forty hours a week, it's even more important to people who live together.

Now that David and I have figured out that extraverts and introverts jump into conversations at completely different points, we can help rather than hinder each other's decision-making process. Realizing that my stated desire to adopt a child was a conversation opener, David began to explore the possibilities with me. We attended information sessions at several adoption agencies. We read books. We examined our budget. We talked. David came to appreciate my feeling-based values, and I came to understand his thinking-based cautions.

Not long ago a friend asked us if we might be interested in adopting a particular infant. "Well, no," I said. "I don't think it would be wise at this time."

"Yes," said David. "This could be just what we've been waiting for."

We looked at each other in amazement—I was speaking the thinking language, and he was speaking the feeling language! Needless to say, the decision has not yet been made. As a perceiving type, I can't say that I mind. There are always new options to explore.

CHAPTER 9

Discipline Your Children Effectively

I T'S a dirty job, but somebody's got to do it.

If that's how the word *discipline* strikes you, then your heart is probably in the right place. I would worry about a parent who enjoyed punishing the kids; and to most people, discipline and punishment are synonymous.

Actually, *discipline* didn't originally mean punishment at all. Even today, if you look the word up in a dictionary, you will find punishment near the end of the definitions. *Discipline* comes from the same root as *disciple,* and *disciples* are what students used to be called. To discipline, then, is to teach.

At some point between the Roman Empire and the twentieth century, *discipline* became a euphemism. Fathers in ancient Rome had the right of life or death over their offspring, and it didn't seem to bother them to exercise it. But beating up one's young fell out of fashion, even though a lot of parents continued to do it. It sounded bad to say, "I just creamed little Hector." So instead the parent said, "I just taught little Hector a lesson;" i.e., "I disciplined him."

And that's roughly how *discipline*, which is a perfectly good word meaning "to teach," came to be applied to one of the less successful teaching methods ever invented by distraught parents.

This chapter, nevertheless, will be partly about punishment. It will also be about authority, self-control, and independence. A well-disciplined child is a joy to be around. It is also the only kind of child that one can safely turn loose on the world.

The book of Proverbs says, "Train a child in the way he should go, and when he is old he will not turn from it" (22:6). That's talking about discipline ("train"), and it's also talking about personality type. Literally, "in the way he should go" means "according to the child's way," and many commentators say the verse is demanding respect for the child's individuality. There are no guarantees if you try to train your child in the way some other child should go. Knowing your child's way, then—the kind of person he or she is—is the first step in good discipline.

Proceed with Caution

This does not mean that to discipline a child effectively you must be sure of the child's exact personality type as measured by the MBTI. In the first place most children's types are not yet one hundred percent obvious; and the younger the child, the more difficult it can be to figure out his or her type. In most cases the child's type is not crystal clear until a great deal of discipline has already been done (or left undone).

Second, even a "textbook case"—a child who seems to be a living example of a particular type description—should not be forced into a mold. Inborn personality type may not change, but children's behavior certainly does; and adults need to give children the freedom to experiment with different styles.

Four Reasons Children Misbehave

Children misbehave for many reasons, but a common denominator is often this: they feel their needs aren't being met. Since children of different types and temperaments have different needs, an understanding of personality differences can help parents deal with their children's inappropriate behavior. This list is based on Keirsey's four temperaments.

1. "I won't stand for being penned up, watched, and told what to do all the time. I'm going to do what I want, no matter what they say."—SP (Need: Freedom)

2. "I don't know what is expected of me. I'm going to test their limits until I find the ones that really hold."—SJ (Need: Security)

3. "Their rules don't make any sense. Why should I pay any attention to them?"—NT (Need: To Understand)

4. "They don't really love me, so it doesn't matter how I act. Maybe if I hurt them, they will begin to pay attention to me."—NF (Need: Affection)

Third, no individual, whether child or adult, matches his or her type description in every detail. An ESFP is like other ESFPs in some respects and unlike them in others. A type description is a pattern that helps us understand others, but it is not an individualized profile. After all, there are only sixteen type descriptions to apply to billions of people.

So be careful as you consider the best ways to discipline your children. If the approaches recommended for their types and temperaments fit them and make your life together easier, use them. If not, keep experimenting.

And remember that anyone who advises you to treat all your children alike either is assuming that they all have identical personalities or has little understanding of what motivates human beings. Don't treat your kids alike—treat them as they need to be treated. That's not far removed from practicing the Golden Rule.

Different Children, Different Needs

Children of different types and temperaments have different needs. Look at the difference temperament makes: an SP craves freedom, an SJ requires security, an NT wants understanding, and an NF looks for meaning.

Perhaps thirty to forty percent of all children are SPs. They take in information through their senses more often than through intuition, and they prefer to interact with the world through their senses as well. These children are often alert and observant. They enjoy adventure, exploration, and games. Above all else, SP children want freedom. With overprotective, authoritarian parents and a tightly regimented school, young SPs are miserable.

Rod was an SP boy with three strikes against him. His father, a minister, was a staunch SJ. His mother, if anything, was an even stauncher one. And the church to which they belonged, if churches could take personality indicators, would certainly have come out SJ. When Rod performed daring bicycle stunts while riding at top speeds down steep roads, his parents took away his bike. When he took off exploring with his friends and came home a half hour late, they grounded him. And when his exuberant behavior was seen as violating some of his church's lifestyle codes, his parents insisted on accompanying him wherever he went for a month.

Before the month was over, Rod turned up missing. The police found him a week later, three states away, working in construction. Only sixteen, he could have been forced home—but his parents suspected they could no longer hold him. They decided to give him the freedom he had been desperately seeking all his life.

Rod's reaction is not unusual among SP children who feel blocked at every turn. These children, often cheerful and friendly, are happy to relate to others if they are treated more or less as equals and given plenty of elbow room. If they feel caged, though, they will kick at the bars until they can make a break for freedom.

SJ children, also making up thirty to forty percent of the population, react to life much differently than SPs. Conducting their lives with their judging function, either thinking or feeling, they actually like their cages. In fact, they feel uncomfortable if they don't know exactly where the limits are.

Heather, an SJ two-year-old, was reprimanded by her mother for picking her nose in public. "If you must pick your nose," her mother said, "go to the bathroom and do it privately." Heather complied; in fact, she made a game of taking elaborate leave of her mother, going into the bathroom, shutting the door, and eventually reappearing with a look of accomplishment on her face. The day after Heather learned this valuable social skill, her mother took her to visit an elderly friend. When they were ushered into the living room, Heather looked about in alarm. In a ringing voice, she asked, "Where may I pick my nose?"

SJ children respect authority, and they often work hard to earn their parents' and teachers' approval. If they misbehave, they expect to be punished; in fact, they may be so uncomfortable if punishment does not follow their offense that they continue to misbehave until it does. To SJ children, parents show they care by enforcing the rules.

Kathy, a teenager with two SJ parents, invited Marilyn to her house one Saturday afternoon. She was surprised that Marilyn did not have to check with her parents before accepting the invitation. Midway through the afternoon, the two girls decided to do a little shopping. Before letting them take the car, Kathy's parents insisted on knowing where they were going, what they were going to do there, and when they would be back. It was Marilyn's turn to be surprised. As they were leaving, she said, to Kathy, "I wish my parents checked up on me that carefully. Then I'd know they really loved me." Marilyn was expressing the SJ's need for security.

NT children, representing only ten to fifteen percent of the population, have quite different needs. These children are often easy to live with because they see no need to create storms over trivial matters. On the other hand, they are not easy to budge once they take a stand. Like T. S. Eliot's Rum Tum Tugger, an NT "will do / As he do do / And there's no doing anything about it!"[1] As the mother of an NT told me, "I never need to fear that Andy's going to be led astray by his friends. If he wants to go wrong, it will be entirely his own choosing!"

NT children, like SP children, are not impressed by authority figures. Position means little to NTs. Whether a person is president, pastor, or parent, he or she has to *earn* an NT's respect by being logical, reasonable, and fair. And that is the key to disciplining NTs: Be willing to explain your requests and rules. An NT's father was overheard saying, "Do as you are told, or accept the consequences." His son immediately responded, "What are the consequences?" The very worst thing to say to a child of this type is "Because I said so."

NF children, with their combination of intuition and feeling, are often idealistic. They may fight for their rights or those of others, but they are easily wounded in battle. Unlike the tougher NTs, they *can* be influenced—by their peers and by their parents. About ten to fifteen percent of all children are NFs.

A mother with three children—an SJ, an NT, and an NF— explained the differences: "If I punish the SJ child, she changes her behavior. With the NT child, punishment doesn't seem to make much difference—unless he thinks I've been unfair. Then he turns absolutely beastly. I don't know how to punish the NF. She seems so wounded by the slightest reprimand that I don't dare punish her more severely. And yet she needs correction just as often as the others."

In general, NFs try to please the adults with whom they live and study. Since they also try to please their agemates, though, conflict may erupt if parents disapprove of their friends. NFs thrive when they know their parents are crazy about them and when they are given enough freedom to pursue their own idealistic goals.

Different Parents, Different Approaches

If kids are different, so are parents. Chances are you have been saying to yourself (fill in the blanks with the appropriate temperament or type), "An _____ I could understand, but what could I ever do with an _____ ?"

SJ parents often have well-ordered households. They see themselves as captains of the ship, and they expect willing compliance from the crew. They know exactly how they want their children to behave, and they usually discipline them consistently. SJ parents are likely to use spankings to enforce their policies.

Parents who are not SJs are less likely to want to exert their authority. Unless their society or church teaches them otherwise, they are not likely to see the home as a hierarchy with Dad on top, Mom either next to him or just below him, and the kids at the bottom. Instead, they may see themselves as tutors (NT), buddies (SP), or friends (NF).

SP parents often like to give their children independence. They are not likely to have a lot of rules and regulations for the children to follow, and their methods of discipline may be rather haphazard. In fact, they may try to avoid using any kind of punishment at all.

NT parents usually try to be fair with their children. They like to give the children as much responsibility as they can handle. Believers in cause and effect, they are often attracted to discipline by logical consequences—letting the children bear the results of their own misbehavior.

NF parents tend to identify with their children. More than the other types, they long for communication, sharing, and harmony. They often hate punishing and are likely to try to get their way through persuasion or rewards.

Fortunately, parents do not have to share their children's temperament in order to discipline them effectively. All children need a balance of freedom and security, understanding and affection. All parents are equipped to meet all four needs to some degree—especially if they realize that some children need more in one area, while others need more in another.

If you and your children enjoy each other's company most of the time, you're obviously doing something right. As the backwoods philosopher advised, "If it ain't broke, don't fix it." But if your children ever respond to you with rebellion, indifference, hostility, hurt, or confusion, you may want to check up on your methods. Are you allowing your SP children enough freedom? Do you provide security in the form of predictable expectations for your SJs? Do you give good explanations for what you require of your NTs? Do your NFs feel loved right down to their bones?

Personally, I'm wary of experts who say I should or should not spank, should or should not withhold privileges, should or should not employ logical consequences as means of training my children. First, the focus of discipline should not be consistently negative—what to do if discipline-as-teaching breaks down. Second, any parent with more than one child needs more than one method of repairing the damages. In fact, even one child needs different responses for different misbehaviors.

When discipline breaks down and a child needs to be restored to full functioning in the family, no formula can tell the parent how best to accomplish the restoration. Parenting is an art, not a science, and art by its very nature is unpredictable. The parent can only ask these basic questions and then proceed in faith:

1. Knowing what I do about this child's personality, how is he or she going to respond if I do this?

2. Will this response include a change for the better in the child's behavior?

3. Will the change be temporary or long-lasting?

4. Will my action help the child learn self-discipline, or will it keep the child dependent on me?

This four-point quiz does not have a key because the answer depends on you, your child, and the situation.

Self-Discipline: The Most Important Lesson

And now we come to the most important aspect of discipline: teaching children to discipline themselves.

In her book *Gifts Differing*, Isabel Briggs Myers included an excellent chapter on helping children learn self-discipline, which she called *good judgment:* "the ability to choose the better alternative and act accordingly."

"What children need is the conviction that *satisfaction can and must be earned,*" wrote Mrs. Myers. Spoiled children do not realize that it *must* be earned; they blame their problems on outside forces beyond their control. These children need to learn that their own actions are largely responsible for what happens to them. "When children knowingly do the wrong thing, the consequences should be consistently disagreeable. Under such conditions, they learn to obey the spoken word and the known rule in the same spirit that they obey the law of gravity, under a similarly mild but inevitable penalty, and at the same time, fifteen months or younger."[2] Dr. Kevin Leman in *How to Make Your Children Mind Without Losing Yours* calls this approach *reality discipline.*

Discouraged children, by contrast, do not realize that satisfaction *can* be earned; feeling like failures, they quit trying. "Both home and school should provide [children] with the experience of doing particular things well and thereby earning the satisfaction they crave," wrote Mrs. Myers. "Because the various types have different gifts and needs, the specific things and satisfactions cannot be the same for all children."[3]

Dr. Jim Dobson in *Hide and Seek* suggests building children's self-esteem by helping them achieve in areas of importance to them, whether math, tennis, or clothing selection. Children who know they can earn satisfaction for themselves are unlikely to expect others to hand it to them on a platter. And imparting this knowledge is as much a part of discipline as spanking or grounding, because self-confident children tend to discipline themselves.

Think about it: Your children will be living with you for no more than eighteen or twenty years. For maybe a third of that time, they are likely to be as big as you are. For three-quarters of the time, they will spend at least half their waking hours at school, not at home. Your opportunities to discipline them are severely restricted. If they do not develop skills in self-discipline, preferably while they are still preschoolers, all too soon they will be set adrift with no compass and no map.

This is true whether they prefer using their perceiving function (S or N) or their judging function (T or F), whether they use perceiving or judging to run their outer lives. As one mother told her daughter, "Being an ENFP does not excuse you from cleaning your room."

Judging is not more important than perceiving. A person who makes judgments without first taking time to perceive is likely to be a bigot. To teach children to use good judgment, parents must use good perception so they know how best to approach the children.

Disciplining children is far more than punishing or controlling them. It means preparing them to separate from us and live productively and happily under their own self-discipline. It includes studying them to learn what makes them tick, considering each situation with a view to how our actions will affect their future, and acting in the way that seems best.

Discipline is a process, not a once-for-all achievement. As parents, we all make mistakes—lots of them.

Fortunately, over the course of twenty years we are given many occasions to practice this art of parenting. Mercifully, we do not have to get everything right on the first try. God is forgiving, and so are our children.

1. T. S. Eliot, "The Rum Tum Tugger," *The Complete Poems and Plays* (New York: Harcourt, Brace & World, 1962), p. 153.
2. Isabel Briggs Myers with Peter B. Myers, *Gifts Differing* (Palo Alto, Calif.: Consulting Psychologists Press, 1980), pp. 193-95.
3. Myers, p. 196.

CHAPTER 10

Help Them Succeed in School

BY the time your children are six years old, school is taking up at least half their waking hours Monday through Friday. For some children, this is a wonderful opportunity.

Kara, in fourth grade, can hardly wait for the school bus to stop at her corner each morning. Friendly and popular, she meets her friends on the bus and exchanges secrets and giggles before the bus makes its final stop in front of the elementary school doors.

Once inside, Kara greets her teacher cheerfully, hangs her coat neatly on her appointed hook, and takes her seat (after brushing off any dust the janitor might have missed). When the teacher asks the class to take out their language books, Kara never has any trouble finding hers—all her books, papers, and equipment are neatly arranged in her desk. Kara's homework is almost always done neatly and on time. She usually listens to whatever is going on in class, and on the few occasions when she is reprimanded for whispering, she apologizes to the teacher.

The teacher has rewarded Kara's faithfulness by giving her a large number of gold stars on the class achievement chart. She has also made Kara a monitor: Kara helps collect papers and straighten common study areas.

Kara is a teacher's dream, and according to the law of averages, about twelve students in every thirty-two-student class resemble her. These are the SJs—the practical, sensible, responsible children without whom few teachers would continue year after year in the classroom, particularly since most elementary school teachers are SJs too.

If there are twelve SJs in an average class, of course, there are also twenty children who are not SJs. Assuming that children's personality types follow the same pattern as adults', that average class would also include twelve SPs, four NTs, and four NFs. Dr. Elizabeth Murphy and Dr. Charles Meisgeier, working directly with children, found a different pattern of type distribution. Based on their figures, we could expect to find, in addition to the twelve SJs, eleven NFs, six SPs, and three NTs.

Since no class is ever average anyway, the actual figures are not so important as the underlying principle: Every class is composed of children of varying personality types, and these children will react to school in completely different ways.

The Other Sixty Percent

Chris, a sixth grader, is an NF. Like Kara, he is friendly and polite. Unlike her, however, he frequently daydreams, his papers are sometimes late, and under his desk lid lurks total chaos. Chris's teacher is fond of him, though, because unlike many boys of his age, he talks easily with adults, expresses appreciation freely, and is gentle with younger children.

Chris's math grades are not wonderful, but he does very well in language arts. A gifted writer, he came up with the idea of putting together a class newspaper, which

---

Four Types of Learners

Dr. Keith Golay, a trainer of school psychologists, has described Keirsey's four temperaments according to their learning styles:

Actual-Spontaneous Learner (SP)

Fun-loving and daring, ASLs are not particularly interested in intellectual matters. For them, the joy is in the doing, and the important moment is now. They learn best from action and hands-on experience.

Actual-Routine Learner (SJ)

Conscientious and responsible, ARLs thrive on structure and predictability. They often form good study habits and memorize well. They learn best when material is presented step by step and when they have time to plan and prepare.

Conceptual-Specific Learner (NT)

Curious and analytical, these serious "little scientists" want to understand how the universe operates. CSLs learn best when they have a problem to solve or when the teacher provides concise, well-reasoned explanations.

Conceptual-Global Learner (NF)

Insightful and person-oriented, CGLs want what they learn to make a difference. Often skilled communicators, CGLs learn best when they believe in what they are doing and when they feel warmth and caring in the classroom.

---

he then edited. He managed to persuade most of the other students to contribute to it, too.

Jonathan, a third grader, is an NT. Eight years old, he has the drive and seriousness of a much older student. He is not rude or troublesome, but he doesn't seem to notice other people. He speaks when spoken to—if he isn't too busy thinking of something else. He does his homework—if he hasn't used up his time on another project he considers more important.

Jonathan's teacher does not know what to do with him. She feels unable to persuade him to do anything but what he wants to do, and what he wants to do is rarely included in her lesson plans. She knows he understands math and science, but she wonders if he is becoming one-sided. His language papers are not great, and he sometimes has a hard time relating to other students.

If classes were composed only of children like Kara, Chris, and Jonathan, teachers' lives would be vastly simplified. Statistically speaking, however, we can expect a class to include from six to twelve children like Pony as well.

Pony is an SP in seventh grade. Even her teacher has a hard time remembering her real name, Penelope. Ever since Pony was three years old, she has spent several hours a day riding, grooming, or training one of the horses her parents raise.

Pony is cheerful and likable. The trouble is, she can't stand school. She hands in no more than half her papers, and most of those are sloppy and incomplete. She simply can't sit still long enough to listen to a teacher's explanations. She tries, but after fifteen seconds her fingers start drumming on the desk. Soon her feet are tapping to rhythms only she can hear, and her eyes glaze over. If the teacher's lecture continues for more than three minutes, Pony starts shifting in her seat, dropping papers and pencils, coughing.

Pony is an expert horsewoman. She's pretty good on the baseball diamond, too. But she's in danger of failing seventh grade, even though the psychometrist who gave her a verbal IQ test reported an above-average IQ.

Pony is an extreme SP, and because she also happens to be an extravert, her dissatisfaction in school is readily apparent. But even quieter or more moderate SPs often find a traditional classroom very trying. It is important for parents and teachers to realize that SP children are just as intelligent as other children, and no more likely to have learning or behavior disorders. They present a challenge in the classroom, though, because their inborn approach to life requires a freedom to experience and experiment that few schools provide.

Different Schools for Different Kids

How can one teacher meet the needs of children of all four temperaments? Dr. Gordon Lawrence, professor of education at the University of Florida in Gainesville, finds the key in MBTI type theory.

Lawrence points out that each of the four preferences measured by the MBTI gives valuable information about students. "The extraversion-introversion preference shows the broad areas of students' *natural interests;* . . . the sensing-intuition preference reveals basic *learning style differences;* . . . the thinking-feeling dimension shows patterns of *commitments and values*; . . . and the judging-perceiving dimension shows *work habits.*[1]

Not only do the preferences make a difference in students, Lawrence points out; they also affect how teachers approach their classrooms. Predictably, extraverts are more attuned to the classroom situation; introverts, to the ideas they are trying to get across. Sensing types tend to emphasize facts and skills; intuitives, the implications of those facts. Thinking types often make objective comments about student performance (i.e., scores and totals); feeling types, subjective comments (i.e., praise and censure). Judging types are more likely to have structured, orderly classrooms; perceiving types, open, group-oriented ones.[2] Although good teachers come in all types, it is not surprising that elementary and junior high school teachers lean toward E, S, F, and J.

Kara, the fourth-grade ESFJ, gets along marvelously in the structured, friendly classroom run by her very competent ESFJ teacher. Janelle, however, had a different experience in her school, even though she is also an ESFJ.

In Janelle's suburban school district, one elementary school was opened up for experimentation. Desks in rows were replaced by study tables and learning centers. Students were encouraged to get involved in whatever interested them, from gerbils to computers. Teachers circulated among students offering commendations, suggestions, and ideas for further projects.

At first Janelle's parents were pleased to be living near this state-of-the-art school. What could be better for their obviously intelligent daughter than individualized instruction carried out to the *n*th degree?

But before long they began to have second thoughts. Formerly a sunny, outgoing little girl, Janelle began to withdraw and pout. The first teacher's evaluation (the school didn't give grades) reported Janelle's hesitation to get involved in group activities. Janelle began talking about "that dumb school," and her parents privately wondered why she wasn't starting to read.

Summer after first grade was fairly peaceful, but in August Janelle started having nightmares. Concerned, her parents talked with the school psychologist, who recommended placing the little girl in one of the district's traditional schools.

Janelle's nightmares ceased two weeks after Labor Day, and by October she was bringing home books to read. She often admiringly quoted her teacher, and her grade card showed top performance. What made the difference? Janelle needed structure to feel secure. The open classroom left her with more choices than she could handle.

Interestingly, the year Janelle transferred to a more traditional school, Leo, an INFP, transferred out. Its predictable routine was stifling him, and the experimental classroom proved to be just what he needed.

Blooming Where You're Planted

Most students, of course, do not have the option of choosing a school to suit their personality type. Every school district has a few first-rate teachers who, through instincts or training, know how to meet the needs of all sorts of students, but most teachers win some and lose some. What can you do to ensure that your children thrive in school?

First, get acquainted with the teachers and administrators at your children's school. Most of them chose that line of work because they genuinely want to help children learn, and they welcome parental input.

One of our daughters had a difficult year in fourth grade. Wanting to be sure her fifth-grade experience would be positive, we made an appointment with her principal. He listened carefully while we explained her personality type as we perceived it and the classroom environment we thought she needed. As a result of our conversation, he assigned her to the teacher he thought would best suit her. He chose well: Just the other day she said, "You know, fifth grade was one of my best years."

Second, find out how your children's classrooms are run. Most teachers are thrilled when parents volunteer to be room parents or teacher's aides, and all schools have parent-teacher conferences and open houses. Ask teachers, "What do you hope to accomplish with the children this year?" Do their answers center on mastery of subject matter? Relationships? Creativity? Skills? Experiences? How will their aims fit in with your children's needs?

Third, do your best to meet the needs that the school leaves unmet. Some parents do this by educating their children at home. Others find creative ways to supplement their children's classroom curriculum. Let's take a closer look at both options.

What about Home Schools?

An increasing number of parents are opting out of the school system altogether. Rather than enrolling their five-year-olds in public kindergarten, they are teaching them at home. Many continue their "home schools" for an additional year or two or even more.

Home schoolers believe that school classrooms are inefficient. At school it takes seven hours, they say, to cover material that they and their children can master in ninety minutes at home. Once finished with lessons, home-schooled children are free to work, play, read, or follow Mom around. They learn more through these low-anxiety, unstructured, daily-life activities than they could possibly learn in an artificial learning situation, home-school advocates insist.

Since young children develop at different rates, not all are ready for formal education at age five or six. Home-school parent-teachers believe they are better equipped to proceed at an individual child's pace than teachers with thirty-two students could hope to be. By allowing for developmental differences, home schoolers believe they avoid problems that are often misdiagnosed as learning disorders.

In addition, many home schoolers are convinced that the public schools encourage low moral standards and religious skepticism. The longer they keep their children by their sides, they believe, the more likely the children will adopt their convictions.

Is home schooling also a good way to allow for differences in personality type? It all depends.

Home schooling can be a good idea if the parent-teachers recognize their children's needs and know how to provide for them.

It can be particularly helpful to young SP children, who love to take things apart, put them together, dig them up, and experience them—but who dislike sitting still for long.

It can be damaging, however, just as public school can be damaging, if parent-teachers attempt to mold their children into their own image rather than providing learning activities geared to the children's learning styles. An ESTJ parent determined to set an ISFP child on the strait and narrow path (as the parent sees it) could be in for some big disappointments.

Conversely, the ISTJ child of an ENFP parent might do better pushing a pencil in a regimented classroom than romping in the fields of golden daffodils envisioned by the parent.

Even so, it cannot be doubted that home schools frequently produce well-educated children. Isabel Myers of MBTI fame had only one year of formal education before entering Swarthmore College at age sixteen, and she is just one of many home-school successes. If your children are young and you feel enthusiastic about teaching them, home schooling is an option to consider.

The Balancing Act

Most parents, of course, do not choose the option of home schooling. Both may work outside the home, or the at-home parent may feel unqualified, uninterested, or downright skeptical of the supposed advantages of educating the kids at home. How can these parents meet the needs left unmet by the school?

By supplementing what the school has to offer.

Do your children sit in rows, fill out worksheets, and line up for recess? Then forget about educational extracurricular activities and send them out to play. Even if they are among the forty percent who thrive in a structured classroom, they need the balance of unstructured hours. At school they can learn to exercise their judging function; at home they can learn to perceive.

Do your children have a lot of freedom at school to choose their own activities? Are they encouraged to move about, to participate in group discussions, to make things? Then don't apologize for spending some after-supper time doing multiplication drills, practicing spelling words, or reviewing the state capitals. This too is part of education.

Exposing children to a wide variety of learning experiences is important. Perhaps even more important is teaching children to do one or two things very, very well.

This is especially important for SP children, whose school experience may leave them frustrated and angry. SPs often get bad grades, but this is not because they lack intelligence. Their abilities are as great as anyone else's. What they frequently lack is the opportunity to use their skills in the practical, hands-on way that is comfortable for them.

Most teachers have stories about the child—usually a boy—who could not read until he got interested in doing something and found he needed further information. Whatever the task—mastering a sport, repairing machinery, constructing fine furniture—the SP learns to do it by doing it, not by listening to a teacher or reading a book. The authority is consulted only after the task is well under way.

Trying to force SP children into an SJ mold is pointless. Many of them simply *cannot* learn in the orderly, progressive, structured way so dear to the SJs. They must be left free to build, fix, play, tinker, experience. Only then will their learning begin, and only then will they have a chance to achieve excellence.

All children—whatever their personality type or temperament—need to feel that they are experts in some area. Lucky the children whose parents perceive their interests, their strengths, and their learning styles and then make it possible for the children to develop their own gifts in their own ways!

The word *education* means "to draw out; to lead." It does not imply changing children into something they are not. Instead it means taking children as they are and using their inclinations, strengths, and preferences in order to draw out from them the very best that they can give.

1. Gordon Lawrence, *People Types and Tiger Stripes: A Practical Guide to Learning Styles,* 2d ed. (Gainesville, Fla.: Center for Applications of Psychological Type, 1982), pp. 38- 39.
2. Lawrence, pp. 79-80.

CHAPTER 11

Give Them What They Need Most

LAST school year our family and a South American family exchanged daughters. We sent the Serranos our sixteen-year-old INTJ Molly, and they sent us their eighteen-year-old ESFJ Adriana. Both girls had a wonderful year making new friends, practicing English and Spanish, and becoming part of new families that truly loved them. The first weeks, however, were rough.

One fall day Adriana helped me understand what each girl was going through. She came into my study carrying a letter from her mother and laughing. Apparently Adriana had told her mother that Americans were cold and distant and unfeeling. This is what Mrs. Serrano, who knew many Americans and did not quite share her daughter's opinion, wrote back:

> I understand what you say about North Americans: they take a long time to show that they love you. Molly has been here only two weeks, and already she has dozens of friends. That is the way we treat people here. You will be lonely for a while, but

eventually you will make friends. North Americans aren't really unfriendly, but they are slow.

Do not think you are the only foreigner with problems, though. Molly is having her own problems with us. She likes our South American warmth and friendliness, but she wishes we would keep appointments. Three times in the last week she has arranged to meet a friend, only to have the friend fail to show up. This is bothering her a lot.

As an ESFJ, Adriana needs people. She loves to do nice things for the people she loves, and she longs to be loved in return.

As an INTJ, Molly needs order and control. She enjoys planning, whether for tomorrow's activities or for law school in four years, and she wants her plans to work out in reality.

Both girls had found ways to meet their needs in their own cultures. Two thousand miles from home, however, both had to find new ways to meet these deep-seated needs.

Fortunately Adriana eventually made friends—unusually quickly by North American standards. Her own warmth and caring, not to mention her striking good looks, attracted her blond classmates, and our phone line grew increasingly busy as the year progressed.

Equally fortunately, Molly learned how to interpret South American time. "If the meeting is at seven," she wrote, "you plan to leave at eight, actually arrive at nine, and wait for it to begin at ten." Molly's inborn need for punctuality and control simply had to give way to the culture in which she found herself—and she learned that it is possible to enjoy life as it comes.

Not all children have mothers as wise as Adriana's, and not all find themselves in challenging situations that force them to face and fulfill their own needs. Many children grow up feeling somewhat uncomfortable, restrained, awkward, or unappreciated, without knowing

---

Four Ways to Raise Your Home's Acceptance Level

1. Turn to the appendix and read the description of the personality type that is your exact opposite. If you are an INTJ, for example, read about ESFPs. Do you live with someone who fits that description in some points? Can you allow that person to be himself or herself, even if this means being radically different from you?

2. Make a list of characteristics you don't like about yourself. On a bad day mine might say *careless, moody, demanding,* and *fickle.* Do any of your children share any of these negative traits? How do you react to that? Do you owe any of your children an apology?

3. Make a list of characteristics you think an ideal child would have. How closely does this paragon of virtue match each of your children? Now list the characteristics you think an ideal parent would have. Are you anything like this mythical person? Are you willing to accept your children as they are, if they are willing to take you in your present state?

4. Make a list of each of your children's strong points. If your memory needs prodding, read their type descriptions as you think about their attitudes and behavior. Post this list where you (and only you) can read it every day. At least once a day, affirm each child for one of his or her strengths.

---

just what is the matter. It may simply be that they have not found good ways to meet their own legitimate needs.

People of different personality types have different needs. If we do not recognize our needs, we are unlikely to meet them. If we do not recognize our children's needs, we cannot help them develop the attitudes and skills that will make them satisfied and productive.

Accepting Differences—and Similarities

No matter what a child's personality type, he or she needs to feel unconditionally accepted by at least one other person. Ideally, acceptance comes from both parents, from siblings, from other relatives, from friends, from school, from church, and eventually from work. In reality, though, most children feel at best only partially accepted even by those who love them the most. How often they hear the refrain—

"If you'd study a little harder, you could get grades just as good as Holly's."

"Jennifer always says thank you without being reminded."

"Look at your half of the room! If Dan can pick things up, why can't you?"

Why is it often so hard to accept our children the way they are, warts and all? Often it is because of their personality types and ours. Either we are so *different* that we totally misunderstand each other, or we are so *similar* that we can't stand to see our own faults repeated in our children.

When I was growing up, my family and I had a major difference in the area of neatness and order. Left to themselves, my parents and my brother had no trouble in this area. They walked through rooms and the pillows stood up and saluted, cobwebs dissolved, and stray sweaters and sneakers scurried into their proper places.

But when I came along, the situation changed. Small shoes began appearing in the middle of the living room. Books left the shelves and stayed opened on the coffee table. Dishes started to linger by the sink, and lights forgot to turn themselves off.

My mother was completely baffled. If Harold could keep his toys neatly lined up on open shelves, why couldn't I? If his clothes could hit the hamper, why couldn't mine? Over a twenty-year period, we had a number of spirited discussions about the neatness issue. Then I left home, married, and had children of my own.

My daughter Heidi and I are both ENFPs. This means that our preferred function is intuition, and our second-favorite function is feeling. (See p. 43, "Two Ways to Find Out Your Dominant Function," for a quick review of the order of functions.) That leaves thinking and sensing in third and fourth places, and those are precisely the functions that seem to help people keep things clean and orderly. When Heidi was ten, we named her room "The Black Hole" because once things entered it they were never seen again.

Now if my ESFJ mother and I had trouble over neatness because we are so *different,* you would think my ENFP daughter and I would see eye-to-eye and live together in disorderly harmony because we are so *similar.* Unfortunately, this has not always been the case.

Over the years I have developed an appreciation for neatness, even if I find it next to impossible to achieve. I have begun putting my best efforts into maintaining an attractive, reasonably hygienic home environment. This is extremely difficult, and my batting average is not 1000. But I persist.

Heidi's similarity to me has irritated me more often than it has called forth my compassion. I have seen it not as childish carelessness, but as willful sabotage. This, of course, is ridiculous, and Heidi deserves a medal for taking my tirades as sweetly as she does. It just goes to show that mere similarity of personality type is no guarantee of acceptance.

If some parents have trouble accepting their children because they are different, while others have trouble accepting their children because they are similar, surely the situation could be reversed! How about accepting our type-alike kids because we understand them and empathize with them, and accepting our type-different kids because they have strengths where we have weaknesses?

It is not always easy for parents to accept their children, but it is the only wise approach. A child who feels totally accepted feels secure enough to behave well, to develop his or her strengths, and to reach out in love to others.

Besides, you might as well accept your children.

Lack of acceptance never changes them for the better. It only makes it harder for them to reach their full potential. Heidi did not start keeping her room clean until I stopped nagging her about it. Once I put her completely in charge of her own turf, she began cleaning it thoroughly once a week. Children who know they are accepted as they are have the freedom to become all they can be.

What Children Want to Be Appreciated For

One of the best ways to communicate acceptance to our children is by appreciating them. Not all appreciation is equally effective, however.

Children of different temperaments may want to be appreciated for different things:

> an SP for a good performance,
> an SJ for faithfulness to duty,
> an NT for a clever insight or solution,
> an NF for himself or herself.

Different personality characteristics may also influence the way children want appreciation expressed:

> an extravert likes public acclaim,
> an introvert likes private affirmation,
> a judging type likes to be given more responsibility,
> a perceiving type likes to be given a break.

When Gary and Margaret Hartzler of Type Resources, Inc., asked over a hundred adults what they like to be appreciated for, they discovered that people of all personality types wanted appreciation in four basic categories. Everyone wanted recognition for achievements, abilities, actions, and attitudes.

Achievements. In virtually the same words, people of all types from ESTJ to INFP reported that they liked to be appreciated for "a job well done."

Children also want recognition for their good work—and that is a good argument for giving them jobs to do. Many household jobs can be attractive to sensing children: straightening beds, setting the table, dusting the living room. When they see the beauty and order their work has created, they feel rewarded, and when their parents add their praises, they know they are appreciated.

The same jobs may not hold intrinsic attraction for a young intuitive, but they can be adapted by encouraging the child to find better ways of accomplishing them. Intuitive children often enjoy cooking, especially if they are allowed to experiment; and they may like some aspects of pet care.

Thinking-type children are often gifted at setting things in order—closets, drawers, or even garages. Feeling-type children may be talented at child care or serving guests.

When children do a job well and know their parents are grateful or proud, they have a strong incentive to do the next job just as well.

Abilities. People of most types reported that they like appreciation of their competence and their intelligence. In other words, they want respect.

Respect is absolutely vital to NT children, but other children thrive on it as well. If we think our children are competent, we trust them and give them responsibilities. If we think they are intelligent, we listen to them and encourage them to make their own decision.

It's easy to see how important respect is when we look at its opposite. If parents think their child is incompetent and stupid, the child has a real problem. A lot of parents who respect their kids, however, never get around to letting them know it—and the effect can be almost as bad as if the parents didn't respect them.

Actions. Almost all personality types want to be appreciated for their kind actions toward others. In the Hartzlers' survey, many respondents used words such as *thoughtfulness, kindness,* and *helpfulness.*

We might think that feeling types, with their emphasis on the personal and the subjective, would put higher value on thoughtfulness than the thinking types, with their fondness for logic and analysis. This is not necessarily the case, and it would be a mistake to overlook a thinking child's attempts to help.

A thinking child and a feeling child may both wish to be appreciated for their kind deeds. The kind of thanks they prefer, though, may differ. Some family counselors advise parents to praise the deed, not the child. This is absolutely correct if they are dealing with thinking children, who may become rather uncomfortable with personal praise. Feeling children also like to have their good deeds praised, but they can handle more generalized tributes as well. When Grandma says, "You're such a thoughtful little girl," the feeling child feels good. As one ENFP wrote on the survey, "Actually, I most like to be appreciated for anything!"

Attitudes. Many thinking types as well as feeling types said they wanted to be appreciated for their attitudes of compassion, understanding, or caring.

If you are the parent of small boys or children of either sex in junior high, you may suspect that the survey does not apply to them. However, it very well might.

When do you hesitate to show that you care? Is it when you fear rejection or ridicule? Think back to your own pre-teen years and experience again what your children are going through. It's tough to be known for being compassionate in today's schools.

Nevertheless, little hints of empathy and understanding will sneak past the strongest barriers from time to time, and when you catch your child in a softer moment, let your appreciation show. It's a good way to reinforce attitudes that the child will soon want and need.

Special cases. Everyone wants appreciation for achievements, abilities, actions, and attitudes. Sensing types also want recognition for their dependability and common sense. Don't take these sterling qualities for granted. Not all children have them to the same degree, and those who excel in practical responsibility deserve their reward.

Similarly, intuitives crave recognition for their creativity, innovation, and imagination. It may be hard for parents to realize that the four-year-old who dumps cinnamon into the mashed potatoes may eventually be a four-star restaurateur, but creativity always starts with the new and the untried. Praise the experimental spirit even as you gently slide the potatoes toward the garbage disposal. Or add eggs, flour, and sugar and make potato pancakes. They're great with applesauce!

How to Show Appreciation

We've looked at a possible difference between feeling types and thinking types in how they like appreciation shown to them. Basically, though, all types like three standard ways of showing appreciation:

Tell the child he or she is appreciated. You can do this directly, through a note, or over the telephone. You don't have to make a production of it; a lot of survey respondents wrote, "A simple thank you is enough."

Hug the child. Everyone likes to be hugged—introverts as well as extraverts, thinking types as well as feeling types. Of course, some survey respondents qualified their answer by adding "if appropriate," and mothers of certain reserved high school boys might not want to give them bear hugs in front of the whole student body. Still, most parents err on the side of too few rather than too many hugs. Some people believe we need several hugs a day just to survive. Why send our kids elsewhere to get them?

Give the child a reward. Rewards come in many forms: money, gifts, extra privileges. While all children like rewards, not all respond equally well to the same kinds.

Isabel Myers urged parents to reward their children with "whatever furnishes the strongest incentive to the child, for example, extra pleasures or possessions for a sensing child, special freedoms or opportunities for an intuitive, new dignity or authority for a thinker, and more praise or companionship for a feeling type."[1]

There are some differences to keep in mind when showing appreciation to children of different types. An extraverted child often enjoys public acclaim and applause, which might embarrass an introverted child beyond recovery. Many introverts prefer a private word of thanks—or even a letter. This is not a hard and fast rule, though; some introverts are quite comfortable in the spotlight.

Feeling types are often motivated by a strong desire to be loved. If this is the case, the best response to a feeling child's achievement or action, ability or attitude may be an outpouring of affection.

Almost all types reported that they show appreciation by "doing things"—sending a card or a gift, baking brownies, preparing a meal. Several commented that this is much easier for them than expressing their thanks verbally. Only a few, however, said that they want people to show appreciation to them by doing things.

Take this as a warning: Your children may not understand the meaning of those chocolate chip cookies unless you tell them. On the other hand, when your kids do something nice for you, realize that they may be saying thank you. Accept their gifts as acts of love, and get an appreciation cycle started.

Meeting Needs Through Appreciation

During Adriana's first semester with us, her psychology teacher administered the MBTI to the class. Adriana came home with a print out describing the behaviors and needs of ESFJs. One paragraph stood out on the page. ESFJs, it said, often show their love by making or doing something. If their love offering is slighted, they are devastated. If it is accepted with enthusiasm and gratitude, they flourish. "Remember that," I told myself.

Shortly thereafter, Adriana baked us some Colombian delicacies. They were very good, and I complimented her warmly—more warmly than is my habit, since I tend to be rather absent-minded about food and drink and other items dear to the hearts of sensing types. Adriana glowed.

From then on, she frequently did small favors or made or bought things for us. We always responded with enthusiasm. And all of us felt very, very good.

I wish I had learned about appreciating ESFJs sooner. As it happens, that's my mother's type. Years ago, when our second daughter was born, she took up temporary residence in an apartment across the hall from ours and helped us enormously. I appreciated her contribution, but I sensed that something was wrong. She didn't seem very happy, somehow.

So I tried something. "You know," I said, "you're an excellent grandmother." Since I don't often hand out such praise, she looked surprised. "Yes," I continued, "Molly positively adores you. And she behaves well for you too." Mother began to smile. From then on she smiled quite a bit. Whatever misgivings she had been feeling seemed to vanish.

How can we give our children what they most need? First by knowing who they are and accepting them totally, then by letting them know we appreciate them.

Each child is different from every other child, and the total package we accept is different from any other package that could ever come our way. Children want to be appreciated for *their* achievements, abilities, actions, and attitudes—not someone else's. They want that appreciation expressed in a way *they* understand.

But we don't have to be psychologists to figure out how to give our children what they need. Offer them whole truckloads of appreciation. Watch for the smile, the satisfied look, the happy embarrassment that comes when the appreciation hits the spot. The more appreciation you give—in whatever style—the more often you'll reach their hearts.

1. Isabel Briggs Myers with Peter B. Myers, *Gifts Differing* (Palo Alto, Calif.: Consulting Psychologists Press, 1980), p.197.

CHAPTER 12

Help Them Reach Their Full Potential

DR. Brown, a retired professor in his seventies, had just received his MBTI results, and they were ambiguous. He was clearly introverted, sensing, and judging, but his thinking-feeling score was right on the line.

"According to MBTI theory," I explained, "you have an underlying preference for one or the other, even though you may be capable of using both thinking-judgment and feeling-judgment skillfully. In a difficult situation your natural instincts will lead you first to logical analysis if you're a thinking type, to personal values if you're a feeling type."

Dr. Brown wasn't so sure. "I don't like that choice," he said. "My score is exactly where I want it to be. I think it's important to have an equal concern for objective principles on the one hand and subjective considerations on the other. I want to have that kind of balance."

People who are learning about the MBTI often ask, "Aren't these characteristics on a continuum? Wouldn't it be better to be somewhere in the middle, say, between sensing and intuition rather than stuck 'way off on one side?"

Not necessarily. Often when a person has trouble deciding between two functions—S or N, T or F—it is not because of good balance. Rather, the person for some reason has not adequately developed the preferred function. When gathering information, the person wavers between sensing and intuiting, trying first one and then the other and using neither effectively. When making a decision, the person is not sure whether to apply thinking or feeling first, and the decision is made badly or not at all. MBTI experts call this *inadequate type development*.

Dr. Brown's type development, though, is hardly inadequate. Known for his patience, kindness, and genuine concern, he also has a reputation for logical, orderly, and incisive thinking. What's the explanation?

How Personality Type Develops

Although a person is probably born with a particular type that does not subsequently change, over the years he or she develops skills in two or three or even all four functions. This can make a big difference in the person's apparent personality type. In their book *From Image to Likeness,* Harold Grant, Magdala Thompson, and Thomas Clarke take a close look at this process of type development.

According to Grant, Thompson, and Clarke, a preschooler does not show a marked preference for one or two functions over the others. "Up to the age of six—designated by the Christian pastoral tradition as the beginning of the use of reason—it would seem that each child is given the opportunity to gain, through undifferentiated experience, a basic familiarity with all four functions," they write.[2]

At about the time the child starts school, however, one function begins to take precedence, and between ages six and twelve the child pays more attention to it

Four Steps Toward Making a Good Decision

Parents of small children are constantly faced with the need to decide. Should we both work? Should we send our child to preschool? How many children should we have?

Parents of older children add the awesome task of helping their children make sound decisions of their own. What is important in a boyfriend or girlfriend? Should I go to college? What do I want to do with my life?

Anyone who has a decision to make or a problem to solve needs to use all four functions, in this order:[1]

1. Use *sensing* to understand the situation. Look at all the facts. Pay attention to details. Be practical and realistic.

2. Use *intuition* to consider all possible ways to change the situation (that is, ways to solve the problem, actions that can be taken). Don't look for just one way; consider dozens, at least. Say "Why not try . . .?" Capture any passing possibility, no matter how far-fetched.

3. Use *thinking* to examine the alternatives. Look at each possibility you have discovered and figure out just what would happen if you made it a reality. List the pros and cons of each idea. Select several options that look workable.

4. Use *feeling* to evaluate each of the better ideas. Would it help you achieve what really matters to you? How would it affect important people in your life? How would it affect you?

By using all four functions in the decision-making process, you make sure that no forgotten data, possibilities, consequences, or values will come back to haunt you later. You are now in a position to make the decision and act on it.

than to the other three. Some schoolchildren are hands-on sensing types; others, dreamy intuitives; some insist on logic and order in true thinking style; others put personal relationships ahead of all other concerns. The function developed during this period, according to these writers, becomes the person's dominant function.

During adolescence the young person's attention

turns to the second function. The dominant function continues, but it takes the back seat for a while. If the dominant function is in the area of perceiving (sensing or intuition), the adolescent now focuses on a judging function (thinking or feeling); if the dominant function is in the area of judging, he or she will begin developing a perceiving function.

According to Grant, Thompson, and Clarke, some people's development slows down or stops after adolescence. This is unfortunate because two functions still remain to be developed. A growing person, one whose type is developing in a healthy way, turns in early adulthood to the third function. (If the second function—the one developed in adolescence—was a perceiving function [S or N], the third function will be the other perceiving function; if it was a judging function [T or F], the third function will also be a judging function.)

Finally in midlife the truly well-developed person will begin paying attention to the fourth function—the opposite of the function first developed in childhood.

Not all MBTI theorists agree with this developmental pattern in all its details. Nevertheless it is obvious that many successful people are skilled in three or even four functions, using opposite forms of perceiving or judging with apparently equal ease. A good artist, for example, has a keen eye for sense impressions—and also an intuitive grasp of the possibilities inherent in the physical world he sees. A good psychologist sympathetically feels human suffering—and is also able to analyze it in order to explain and treat it.

So what does that mean for parents? Should we encourage our children to develop their dominant function, whatever that may be, during their elementary school years; their second function beginning at puberty? Or should we try to help them achieve balance, a more-or-less equal facility with all four functions?

You Can't Have It All

It is important to help our children develop their first two functions first, until they can use them with ease and skill.

By definition, the dominant function is the form of perceiving or judging that a person prefers to use. Extraverts generally use their dominant function in the outer world. An extraverted sensing type enjoys people, things, and events in the here and now. An extraverted intuitive, by contrast, is always looking for ways to change the present situation for the better. An extraverted thinking type organizes the environment, while an extraverted feeling type uses important values in dealing with it.

Introverts tend to use their dominant function in the inner world. An introverted sensing type looks for the idea behind external reality. An introverted intuitive spins theories. An introverted thinking type creates models and systems, while an introverted feeling type forms ideals and values.

Obviously while a person is immersed in enjoying the present situation, he or she cannot be plotting to change it; and while a person is organizing the environment, he or she cannot also be adapting to it. In most cases it is impossible to use sensing-perception and intuitive-perception at the same time, just as it is impossible to use thinking-judgment and feeling-judgment simultaneously.

That's why children often appear one-sided: They are so busy developing one function that they forget the complementary function altogether.

It's unrealistic to expect a seven-year-old intuitive to know by heart all the Narnia plots and also to remember to put the toilet seat down every time.

It's unfair to scold a five-year-old thinking type for not waxing enthusiastic over a gift for which he has no use.

While a child is engrossed in developing one side of the personality, other sides may get short shrift. Of course parents must patiently persist in teaching intuitives to notice details and sensing types to consider possibilities; of course they must insist that feeling types consider the consequences and that thinking types be polite. But they should not be surprised if these lessons do not stick immediately, and they should not be irritable when the lessons must be repeated.

The Danger of Blocking the Dominant Function

One of the most important jobs in a young child's life is developing the favored function, and parents must be sure nothing stands in the way of that.

Lisa, a clear-cut ESTJ from an early age, enjoyed organizing and directing groups of kids. Forthright more often than tactful, she usually got her way but sometimes left hard feelings in her wake. Lisa's parents were concerned. Their daughter was not the gentle, dainty, retiring little lady they had intended to bring up. By their standards she wasn't very feminine at all. They decided to act.

Lisa definitely needed to have some corners knocked off or at least sanded down. She needed to be told, for example, that people follow more loyally if the leader considers their feelings. She needed to learn more socially acceptable ways of handling disagreements. But her parents weren't content to recognize her gifts of leadership and help her use them more successfully. Instead they tried to change her into someone she was not.

"Ladies don't tell people what to do." "Girls don't lead, they follow." "Let the boys decide what to do." The words differed, but the message was always the same—to gain her parents' approval, Lisa would have to be demure and somewhat passive, like her younger sister. And that's just what Lisa tried to do for twenty years, until two divorces and an emotional collapse forced her to take a long look at who she really was.

Sam, an INFJ, was a dreamy little boy whose inner world was peopled by ghosts, dragons, talking bears, and knights in armor. He loved to read mythology, and he showed considerable talent in writing fantasy stories.
Sam's parents, unfortunately, thought the human imagination was a waste of time and possibly even evil. If they caught Sam writing, they gave him a useful task such as raking leaves or weeding the garden. When he came home from the library, they checked his stack of books to be sure most of them were about astronomy or machinery or some other safe subject.

Sam learned a lot of practical skills, although he never really excelled in them. Over the years he gradually lost interest in writing. Today Sam works as a bank teller. When his small son asks for a story, he says he can't remember any.

Whatever our motives, we damage our children when we stand between them and their preferred function. Conversely, we give them a priceless gift when we help them develop into the persons God intended them to be.

Developing the Dominant Function

The best way to help our children develop their dominant function is to give them access to the resources they need.

Sensing children drink in whatever is in the environment. The more you can enrich that environment, the better. Try:

• living with a little mud so they can sink their hands deep into the spring earth

• taking time for regular excursions to museums

• arranging physical activities such as sports, dance lessons, bike or ski expeditions

• introducing them to tastes and sounds of other countries

Intuitive children have boundless imaginations. They need freedom and room to let their imaginations play. Try:

• introducing them to fantasy in literature and drama

• giving them basic building materials or cooking ingredients and letting them do as they like with them

• encouraging them to make up stories and songs for you

• helping them follow through on projects of their own devising

Thinking children thrive on logic and order. They need problems to solve and challenges to meet. Try:

• asking them for advice in areas where logic and analysis are important (for example, a thinking child might do an efficiency analysis of your household operations and thereby save you a lot of work!)

• providing them with books of math and logic puzzles

• letting them explain the rules of a game to the rest of the family

• sending them for training in computer languages while they are still in the early grades

Feeling children want close personal relationships and family harmony. The more pleased you are with their progress, the more progress they will make. Try:

• sharing activities you particularly enjoy with them

• reading to them about happy families that enjoy each other's company and work well together

• teaching them the basics of child care and helping them find small children to play with, babysit, or teach

• providing them with a responsive pet to love and care for

Developing the Other Functions

Children must be comfortable with their dominant function before they can easily pay attention to the other three functions. Just as a left-handed child is hampered if forced to use the right hand for writing, an intuitive child is handicapped if forced to relate to the world through sensing—and so on down the line.

But that does not mean the other three functions should be ignored. Even if you wanted to ignore them, you couldn't. All of us, children and adults, use all four functions. We have to, to survive. (See page 135 for suggestions on how to use all four functions for effective decision making.)

Remember that it is difficult if not impossible to identify a very small child's dominant function. Even if you were quite sure that your three-year-old was a dominant thinker, for example, you would be restricting his or her development to focus narrowly on logic-based activities. Young children need to be bombarded with sensing, intuiting, thinking, and feeling stimuli. They need to use all four functions, both actively with other children and quietly in the privacy of their rooms. If a small child shies away from using a particular function, that may be the very area the parents need to emphasize—but gently.

Remember too that older children or teen-agers often turn for a time from the dominant function in order to develop the second function. When the child who was formerly lost in Never-Never Land suddenly develops a taste for memorizing baseball scores, parents are understandably confused. Wise parents see adolescence as a time to shift gears, open up new possibilities, explore uncharted territories with their rapidly maturing children.

So while parents need to support their children as they develop their dominant function, they also need to be ready to help them learn how to use the other three as needed.

Children find their second function relatively easy and enjoyable to use (if in doubt about your child's second function, see the description of his or her personality type in the appendix). You can help them develop it just as you help them develop their preferred function, following some of the suggestions above or devising ways of your own. Keep in mind, though, that an extravert uses the second function in the inner world, whereas an introvert uses it in the outer world (just the reverse of the dominant function).

The third and fourth functions may be a different story. Most children are uncomfortable and unskilled in these areas; many adults do not like to use them either. As opposites to the first and second functions, they are unfamiliar and awkward to use.

The secret to using the third and fourth functions is this: Use them as helpers, not directors. Terry, a high-school senior, is an ENTP. His first function is intuition, and he is not very skilled at using sensing. Terry, however, has a wonderful idea for a mystery story. A crime has been committed, and the only six people who could have done it have perfect alibis.

To write his story Terry will have to make heavy use of sensing. He will need to describe the crime and the suspects. He will have to give details about places, events, times. These are things that Terry often does not notice, but he is willing to pay attention to them in order to bring his story to life. Terry is using his fourth function, sensing, in the service of his first function, intuition (which gave him the idea for the story), and his second function, thinking (by which he has worked out the logic for the plot).

Similarly, children who are dominant feeling-types can train themselves to use thinking-type logic if it will help them achieve their personal goals, and children who are dominant thinking-types can take feeling-type values into account by seeing them as factors to be analyzed.

A great deal of the process of child rearing centers on promoting good type development: teaching children to recognize the kind of response appropriate to the situation, and to discipline themselves to respond in that way—even if it takes a bit of effort.

If it sounds like the work of a lifetime, that's because it is. Professor Brown, who could not decide if he was a thinking or a feeling type, has been growing and developing for over seventy years. He now knows when to use sensing and when to use intuition, when thinking is necessary and when feeling is more appropriate. This level of type development is rarely seen before age fifty. For that matter, most senior citizens haven't attained it either. Age sneaks up on all of us, but it takes years of awareness and discipline to achieve maturity.

We can't expect our children to have the wisdom and balance of a Professor Brown, or even of ourselves. But we can start them on the road to good type development by encouraging their natural preferences and by providing them with countless opportunities to use all the other sides of their personality as well.

1. A more complete discussion of this procedure is in Isabel Briggs Myers and Mary H. McCaulley, *Manual: A Guide to the Development and Use of the Myers-Briggs Type Indicator*, 2d ed. (Palo Alto, Calif.: Consulting Psychologists Press, 1985), pp. 65-66.

2. Harold Grant, Magdala Thompson, and Thomas Clarke, *From Image to Likeness: A Jungian Path in the Gospel Journey* (New York: Paulist Press, 1983), p. 20.

CHAPTER 13

Lead Them Gently to God

NEXT time you are in church, look around you at the children. For all their enthusiastic participation in Sunday school now, many will completely give up church attendance within ten or twenty years. Others will attend, but only occasionally; or they will join churches radically different in their approach from yours. What percentage do you suppose will grow up to be active, faithful church members?

It would take a prophet, not a statistician, to provide the answer. One thing is sure, however: A large proportion of parents of adult children carry a perpetual load of grief because their children have rejected their religious roots.

If you are not a Christian, this chapter may seem one-sided to you. I intentionally write from my own Christian perspective because I have found that ideas are communicated most effectively when they can be tied to specific, concrete examples. The MBTI, however, is religiously neutral. It is used successfully with Christians and

Jews, members of eastern religions and agnostics. Whatever your world view, you undoubtedly have deeply held traditions and values you wish to transmit to your children. Please read this chapter in light of your own cherished beliefs, translating where necessary.

One researcher, trying to learn why so many children spurn the faith of their fathers (and mothers), discovered that many teen-age boys turn off religion because of the way it is presented to them. Think about it—if you were thirteen years old, concerned about your sexual identity, wanting to find out what it means to be a man—would you want to "accept Jesus into your heart," "surrender to Jesus," "give your heart to Jesus"? Those terms all reflect the relationship of a woman to a man. They might attract girls or effeminate boys, but they only turn off most young men.

Boys, this researcher concluded, are better served by appeals to discipleship. Jesus himself used this approach with the crowds: "If anyone would come after me, he must deny himself and take up his cross and follow me" (Mark 8:34). Being his disciple involved more than intimacy: "Not everyone who says to me, 'Lord, Lord,' will enter the kingdom of heaven, but only he who does the will of my Father who is in heaven" (Matthew 7:21).

It is true that Jesus wants us to give our hearts to him. It is also true that he wants us to follow him along a difficult path. Truth is not the issue here; the question is rather how to present Jesus so that potential young disciples will *want* to follow him.

Advertisers are in the business of influencing people to want their products. That is why many of them pay close attention to market research into personality types and life styles. If they want to sell a soft drink to well-educated, double-income couples without children, they will use one approach. If they want to sell the same soft drink to first-generation immigrants with large families, they will use quite a different approach.

Four Reasons to Go to Church—
and Some People They Might Appeal To

1. *Action.* As a church member, I can do so much good in the world. I can join with others to feed the hungry, visit the sick, and uphold Christian moral values. Even if I don't actively do these things myself, I can make my witness known by affiliating with people who are on the right side. (Sensing)

2. *Worship.* Most of the time I "see through a glass, darkly," but in prayer I understand realities too deep to express directly. When my soul joins with the "cloud of witnesses" at the Lord's Table, I know who I am and where I am going. (Intuiting)

3. *Study.* Theology is important to me. I want to understand Scripture and see how it all fits together. If I'm going to live by it, it had better make sense to me. (Thinking)

4. *Fellowship.* God is love, and he reveals his love through other people. I go to church to be part of his body, to get and give support, to enjoy the company of others who believe as I do. (Feeling)

And yet many Christian parents, although they want their children to become Christians far more earnestly than any advertiser ever wanted anyone to buy a soft drink, expect one approach to fit all. As Jesus observed, "The people of this world are more shrewd in dealing with their own kind than are the people of the light" (Luke 16:8).

Gifts Differing

The writers of Scripture recognized that people come in wonderfully different packages. In a moving passage from which Isabel Briggs Myers took the title of her book on psychological type, St. Paul wrote:

> Just as each of us has one body with many members, and these members do not all have the same function, so in Christ we who are many form one body,

and each member belongs to all the others. We have different gifts, according to the grace given us. If a man's gift is prophesying, let him use it in proportion to his faith. If it is serving, let him serve; if it is teaching, let him teach; if it is encouraging, let him encourage; if it is contributing to the needs of others, let him give generously; if it is leadership, let him govern diligently; if it is showing mercy, let him do it cheerfully (Romans 12:4-8).

In case anyone missed his point, he made it again in 1 Corinthians 12, an impassioned chapter on the church's need for people of all types—"all sorts and conditions of men," as the Anglican prayer book puts it. Consider his words:

Now the body is not made up of one part but of many. If the foot should say, 'Because I am not a hand, I do not belong to the body,' it would not for that reason cease to be part of the body. And if the ear should say, 'Because I am not an eye, I do not belong to the body,' it would not for that reason cease to be part of the body. If the whole body were an eye, where would the sense of hearing be? If the whole body were an ear, where would the sense of smell be? But in fact God has arranged the parts in the body, every one of them, just as he wanted them to be" (vv. 14-18).

God created people of differing personality types so that his redeeming grace could be felt in all aspects of creation. Unfortunately, congregations often specialize in one type or another, ignoring or criticizing people of other types. And some of those left-out people are our children.

The Institutional Church Personality

Take this quiz: What personality types are most likely to
• conserve treasures from the past?

• fear or dislike unnecessary change?

• believe in law and order and enforce the rules they believe in?

• identify themselves with the institutions or organizations to which they belong?

• be in the majority in conservative Christian churches?

If you answered sensing and judging types, go to the head of the class.

The institutional church seems to be designed with sensing-judging types in mind. It has a rich history. It is often physically beautiful, and its services are likely to appeal to the senses. It emphasizes morality—how people ought to behave. It seems to be one of the few forces holding back the tide of chaos threatening to inundate our modern world.

Studies indicate that sensing-judging types are especially strong in Catholic and conservative Protestant churches. But sensing-judging types make up less than forty percent of the general population, and there is evidence to suggest that they may form an even lower percentage among schoolchildren—perhaps under thirty percent. How might children who are not SJs respond to an SJ-oriented church?

That depends on how the SJs relate to them. Sensing-perceiving types, with their need for freedom and challenge, might feel stifled by the traditions and rules of conventional Christianity and simply stop attending as soon as they are old enough to have some say in the matter. On the other hand, an active, fun-loving youth group might capture their interest and hold them.

Intuitives might grow impatient with the church's emphasis on precedent and tradition, like the intuitive teen-ager who wrote this parody of "Onward, Christian Soldiers": "Like a mighty turtle / Moves the church of God; / Brethren, we can't tread where / No one else has trod." On the other hand, if their ideas are welcomed, intuitives can grow into effective leaders.

Intuitive-feeling types often have a strong need to belong. Like the sensing-judging types, they appreciate their historical roots. They may feel frustrated if their church does not seem to be living up to its high ideals. Some drop out, denouncing the church for hypocrisy. Others attempt to reform or renew the church. A high percentage of pastors are intuitive-feeling types.

Intuitive-thinking types want their church to be run efficiently. They also want its proclamations to make sense. An advertisement produced by the Episcopal Ad Project reads, "There's only one problem with religions that have all the answers. They don't allow questions." NTs must be allowed to explore ideas, even if that means asking uncomfortable questions.

The Trouble with Tyranny

As parents, we naturally hope our children will grow to have a strong faith. We offer them whatever we have found to be true, meaningful, and solid, and we are hurt if they reject it. We may feel they have rejected us personally (especially if we are feeling types), or we may fear that they have compromised their eternal salvation (especially if we are SJs).

In this area, as in so many others, our very zeal may work against us. Ruth, an ISTP, was raised by an ESTJ fundamentalist minister who was determined that she should believe exactly as he did. So when she began to stray slightly from what he saw as the path of virtue, he beat her.

"I'm an atheist," Ruth told me one day over lunch after spending at least an hour talking about her concept of God.

"You're not a very good one," I responded. "You're absolutely consumed by your interest in God."

"Well," she said, "at least I don't believe in my father's God."

By contrast, Tim's family had a rather loose approach to his religious upbringing. An ESFP, he enjoyed getting acquainted with a wide variety of churches in his youth—Baptist, Presbyterian, Christian Reformed, Episcopalian, Catholic. It wasn't that Tim's family didn't know what they believed. They did; but they moved a great deal and chose churches on the basis of what seemed most suitable in their area.

"My dad was afraid my experience would confuse me," said Tim, who continues to attend church regularly. "I don't think it did. Basically, my view of God is very similar to his."

Ruth's parents did not meet her strong need for freedom to explore different ways to think about God. It probably never occurred to them that her needs were any different from theirs. Their motto might have been, "If it's good enough for Grandpa, it's good enough for me—and for you." Tim's parents, probably without realizing it, provided the atmosphere he needed to grow spiritually.

Different Spiritual Needs

What do children of different types and temperaments need? We can expect certain patterns:

Sensing-perceiving types want freedom and often, beauty. The scriptural word that most appeals to them is *liberty*. They love to think of God as Creator, because they revel in his creation. They may enjoy stories about adventurous missionaries, and they may want to do brave deeds or make generous sacrifices for God.

Sensing-judging types want stability and predictability. They are likely to enjoy memorizing Scripture, especially if they are rewarded for their achievement. They like the familiar songs and rituals of Sunday school. Their watchword is *righteousness*. They want to know what God expects of them, and they do their best to perform it.

Thinking types, whether intuitive or sensing, want truth. Firm believers in God's *justice*, they respect churches and individuals who practice what they preach. Intuitive thinking types, even as preschoolers, ask probing questions, and nothing bothers them so much as evasive or simplistic answers.

Feeling types, whether intuitive or sensing, want affiliation. They love Sunday school if they love their teachers—but if their teachers are impatient with them, they may resist going. These children want assurance that God loves them personally, and they are likely to be overcome with guilt if they misbehave. More than anything else, they want *mercy,* both for themselves and for others. Intuitive feeling types, especially if they are introverted, may seek a mystical experience that assures them of God's grace.

Small children do not usually make their personality type obvious. Still experimenting with all four functions, they enjoy active participation coupled with familiar routine, explanations along with hugs.

Once in school, children's preferences become more marked. The kid who can't sit still, the one who always comes prepared, the incessant questioner, the one who idolizes the teacher—these are familiar participants in every Sunday school class.

Note that it doesn't necessarily help a child's popularity to be an SJ or an NF, the two types most likely to be comfortable in church. These children may be nicknamed "Goody Goody," "Sissy," "Crybaby," or "Teacher's Pet." Wise parents and teachers will not heap too much praise on the faithful SJs or the sensitive NFs. Instead, they will find ways for all the children in the class or family to participate. Then all can be appreciated for their own gifts, and no one will need to feel like a misfit.

Sin, Superstition, and the Inferior Function

The MBTI gives out some information that is very helpful in understanding and guiding children's spiritual development. It identifies not only the dominant and second functions, but also the third and fourth functions. The fourth function is the one that is most unattractive; therefore it is the least comfortable one to use. It is sometimes called the *inferior function.* Because the inferior function is hard for us to use, it can get us into trouble. In theological terms, it can even lead us into sin.

The inferior function is the exact opposite of the dominant function. If the dominant function is feeling, the inferior function is thinking. If the dominant is sensing, the inferior is intuiting. If we allow our inferior function to take over and do tasks it is not equipped to handle, we often act foolishly. If we squash our inferior function and refuse to let it help at all, we can also make serious mistakes.

People whose dominant function is sensing can err in two directions. If they give intuition the upper hand, they may begin to imagine all kinds of wild, improbable, and no doubt dangerous possibilities. A small child who is usually practical and sensible, for example, may be persuaded that a burglar is in the closet. If sensing types go to the other extreme and banish intuition altogether, they may put too much faith in the physical, material world. In matters of faith, the unseen is sometimes more important than the seen. Children or adults who do not understand that may become superstitious.

People whose dominant function is intuition need to beware of being overwhelmed by sensing. When this happens, they may become sensitive to detail to the point of being nit-picky. (This may have been the Pharisees' problem.) On the other hand, intuitives must not divorce themselves from sensing. Without it, they risk letting their speculations run wild. (This may have been the problem of the Christian heretics that troubled Peter and Paul.)

People whose dominant function is thinking need to stay alert if their feeling function threatens to take over. In the grip of feeling, they may lash out in anger or display other emotions inappropriately. Still, they need to use feeling to keep their thinking from leading them into skepticism.

People whose dominant function is feeling, when they are tired or out of sorts, may surprise themselves and everyone else by becoming unusually severe and critical. Their inferior thinking function has taken over. If they ignore thinking-judgment, though, they are in danger of falling for any new religious fad that comes along, like the people with "itching ears" Paul mentions in 2 Timothy 4:3.

This inferior function is important for parents to understand. It helps explain occasional outbursts of odd behavior, whether in our children or in ourselves. It also warns us of what can happen if we try to turn our children into something they are not.

The Gifts God Gave Us

If parents or other religious authorities try to persuade children that the only way to God is along the practical, realistic, present-oriented sensing path, the sensing types will shrug and say, "What's new?" The intuitives, however, may conclude that such religion is not worth their time. Why devote themselves to a system that distrusts imagination, suspects poetry, and looks for concrete instructions where Scripture intends to evoke worship?

On the other hand, the parents may succeed. They may convince the intuitive children that their natural way is wrong and that the sensing way is the only one

God approves. What happens if children are forced to live by their inferior function?

They likely won't perform very well. Rather than using data and details competently, as sensing types do, intuitives may use them either incompetently or inappropriately. If they are unable to get adequate information through sensing, they will make uninformed decisions. They may become reactionary and prejudiced. Or if they learn sensing skills in spite of themselves, they may turn into legalists and petty tyrants.

In *Peter Pan* Mrs. Darling slips into her children's room every night after they are fast asleep and rearranges the furniture in their minds. This is a terrible thing for parents to do. In most cases it doesn't work. It leads only to bitter struggles and teen-age rebellion. But when it does work, the results are even worse.

God gave us and our children the personalities he wants us to have. Each psychological function has important contributions to make to the church.

Sensing types bring a firm grounding in reality, a talent for practical matters, unswerving loyalty, a sense of joy in God's creation. They may have the gifts of leadership or serving.

Intuitives bring a vision for the future, enthusiastic anticipation of what God has in store for them, a sense of mystery and holiness. They may have the gifts of preaching or distinguishing between spirits.

Thinking types bring concern for justice, an understanding of theology, a passion for truth. They may have the gifts of prophecy or teaching.

Feeling types bring concern for others' needs, an ability to mediate, an inspiring idealism. They may have the gifts of encouraging or showing mercy.

Our job as parents is not to redesign our children, but to thank God for the way he has created them and to help bring out the best they have to offer. Parenthood doesn't come with a guarantee, and respecting our children's spiritual needs and gifts is not a never-fail map to bring them to God. When we accept our children as they are, however, we help clear the road between them and God. Then they can see him clearly for themselves, and they can respond in the psalmist's words of praise:

> You created my inmost being;
> you knit me together in my mother's womb.
> I praise you because I am fearfully and wonderfully
>   made;
> your works are wonderful,
> I know that full well (Psalm 139:13-14).

POSTSCRIPT

NOW that you have journeyed into the fascinating world of psychological type, you may never be the same again.

You may find yourself guessing the personality types of characters in novels and movies, public figures, people you work with.

You may start explaining type theory to people you have just met at parties.

You may even try typing your pets. (I have been introduced to an INTJ chihuahua-dachshund, an ISFJ Shetland sheepdog, and an ENFP cat.)

Psychological type theory is a serious academic pursuit, of course, but it is also fun. In fact, I tend to mistrust typewatchers who are too solemn.

As you apply your understanding of personality type, keep these things in mind:

Four Facts

1. No type is better than any other type. The best type for you to be is whatever type you are.

2. No type is more intelligent than any other type. Intelligence is not measured by the MBTI.

3. No type is more spiritual or moral than any other type. People of all types are saints and sinners. Most of us are saints and sinners simultaneously.

4. No type is more emotionally balanced than any other type. Mental and emotional health are not measured by the MBTI.

Two Don'ts

1. Do not use type as an excuse for failings. Of course you make mistakes in your weak areas. Why would you make them where you are strong? They are still mistakes, and you still need to change your behavior.

2. Do not use type to stereotype yourself or others. People of the same type may nevertheless be very different from one another.

Three Do's

1. Use type to widen your understanding of human behavior, to help you see the possibilities that exist in all of us.

2. Use type to help you identify areas in which you need to change or develop.

3. Use type to make you more compassionate, more sympathetic with others.

The Golden Rule of Typewatching:

*Use type with others
as you would have others use type with you.*

APPENDIX

I am grateful to Isabel Briggs Myers, David Keirsey and Marilyn Bates, Gordon Lawrence, Harold Grant, and Susan Scanlon for many aspects of these descriptions. See the bibliography for descriptions of their work.

ESTJ
THE BOSS

ESTJs love deciding what should be done, setting up the procedures to be followed, delegating tasks, and managing the operation. They are happiest when their work has immediate, concrete results, and they are likely to get jobs done efficiently and on schedule. Since they enjoy administration and do it well, they are often found in responsible positions.

ESTJs are . . .

Logical: they believe behavior should be based on reason, and they are not moved by appeals to emotion.

Dependable: when they take on a task, they complete it; when they make an appointment, they keep it—on time.

Orderly: detail-oriented, they categorize their ideas, belongings, and time, following routines at home and at work.

Practical: if they see no useful application for an idea, they are not interested in it.

Realistic: they base their decisions on facts and experience.

Conservative: they see no reason to change traditional ways of doing things.

Loyal: they stand by their mates, children, parents, employers, schools, churches, clubs, communities.

Danger zones: ESTJs may make decisions or give orders without taking people's feelings into account. They may lose patience, especially if they think those around them are inefficient, sloppy, or lacking in purpose. They may be prejudiced or judgmental, especially if they do not take enough time to gather information before making a decision. For top productivity, ESTJs need to train themselves to stop and listen to what people are saying, to show appreciation for jobs well done, and to make people's feelings an important factor in their decision-making process.

ESTJ parents are loyal and faithful to spouse and children. They often spend a great deal of time and energy at work, however, and may have trouble finding enough time for the family. Since they love traditions, they may find that their best family time is connected with holidays. They love Thanksgiving dinner, Christmas, and birthdays. They are also likely to be pillars of their church, so if it offers family activities, they will benefit. Many ESTJ parents want their children to be involved in productive activities and will back them with financial and moral support. If ESTJ parents are not careful, though, they may seem unsympathetic to a feeling child or unimaginative to an intuitive child.

ESTJ children are the "leaders of the pack." Alert and observant, they know what is going on in their homes, schools, and communities. They are better organized than many other children, and they enjoy setting goals for themselves (and others). These are strong-willed children who obey when they think their parents and teachers are being reasonable and just. ESTJ children may be respected by their peers and given positions of leadership, or they may be resented and considered "bossy." A lot depends on how well they train themselves to relate to others.

Similar type: ENTJ
Dominant function: thinking
Second function: sensing
Inferior function: feeling

ENTJ
THE EXECUTIVE

ENTJs have a vision, and they are eager to bring it to fulfillment. They love deciding what should be done, setting up the procedures to be followed, delegating tasks, and managing the operation. They are happiest when their work has long-range implications, and they are likely to be expert at removing roadblocks to the accomplishment of their dream. Since they enjoy administration and do it well, they are often found in responsible positions.

ENTJs are . . .

Logical: they believe behavior should be based on reason, and they are not moved by appeals to emotion.

Dependable: when they take on a task, they do it thoroughly and well.

Efficient: they make long-range plans, keep their objectives in plain view, and look for the best way to achieve them.

Future oriented: if they don't have complex problems to solve and possibilities to explore, they lose interest.

Theoretical: they base their decisions on intuition, insights, and hypotheses.

Innovative: they see the present and the known as jumping-off points for what could be brought into being.

Intellectual: they are interested in new ideas, approaches, and theories and can often deal well with complexity.

Danger zones: ENTJs may make decisions or give orders without taking people's feelings into account. They may lose patience, especially if they think those around them are inefficient, stuck in a rut, or lacking in purpose. They may be prejudiced or judgmental, especially if they do not take enough time to gather information before making a decision. To accomplish their aims, ENTJs need to train themselves to stop and listen to what people are saying, to show appreciation for jobs well done, and to make people's feelings an important factor in their decision-making process.

ENTJ parents are in charge of the home, although they often spend a great deal of time and energy at work and may have trouble finding enough time for the family. ENTJs try to use their executive ability to create a productive family system where relationships and physical needs are handled efficiently. Often they believe that with the right system, they will be able to achieve any results they envision. They tend to be firm disciplinarians and to expect their children to achieve. If ENTJ parents are not careful, they may seem unsympathetic to a feeling child or rigid to a perceiving child.

ENTJ children are natural leaders. They seem driven to improve their schools, their homes, their neighborhoods, their world. They enjoy setting goals, making plans, and persuading others to help them achieve them. These are strong-willed children who obey when they think their parents and teachers are being reasonable and just. ENTJ children may be respected by their peers and given positions of leadership, or they may be resented and considered "bossy." A lot depends on how well they train themselves to relate to others.

> Similar type: ESTJ
> Dominant function: thinking
> Second function: intuition
> Inferior function: feeling

ESFJ
THE HOST (OR HOSTESS)

ESFJs love people. They shine at social occasions; they love celebrations in beautiful surroundings with excellent food and drink and warm fellowship. Happiest when they are doing something nice for someone, they are usually able to say whatever is needed to make everyone feel comfortable. They are likely to choose work that lets them interact with others, and they are most effective when they are given plenty of encouragement and approval.

ESFJs are . . .

Expressive: their emotional reactions are usually plainly visible.

Sympathetic: they identify with others, looking for areas of agreement; they love to admire other people openly.

Talkative: they solve their problems and generate ideas by talking; in fact, they enjoy talking so much that they may have a hard time coming to the point.

Devoted: they stick up for people they admire, institutions they respect, or causes they believe in.

Conscientious: they have firm ideals, which they most likely learned from an admired authority figure, and they try to live up to them. They expect their associates to live up to them too!

Cooperative: they love to work with committees on

worthy causes; their obvious good will encourages others to cooperate with them.

Orderly: they take good care of their homes; they keep careful track of the details of everyday life.

Practical: they have little interest in abstract possibilities for the future; they want realistic approaches to today's needs.

Danger zones: ESFJs may try so hard to agree with others that they give up their own beliefs. They tend to ignore things that offend or hurt them, thus denying themselves the opportunity to deal with these problems. They may suffer under a load of guilt if they take the responsibility for maintaining harmony in any group of which they are a part. Their need to nurture is so strong that they may choose an unsuitable mate and try to reform or save him or her. To develop enduring relationships, ESFJs need to use their sensing to check out reality.

ESFJ parents are loyal and faithful to spouse and children. Believers in traditional family values, they want their homes to be warm and well regulated. They love observing traditions and can turn birthdays, anniversaries, and holidays into memorable feasts. They expect their children to uphold their own values and feel personally responsible when they do not.

ESFJ children are friendly, helpful, and obedient. Wanting others to be happy with them, they blossom when praised and wilt when criticized. They may take on more responsibility than they can handle with their limited experience, even to the point of not looking out for their own needs. These children crave affection and order: They must know they are loved, and they must know what to expect. They are often popular, both with their peers and with adults.

Similar type: ENFJ
Dominant function: feeling
Second function: sensing
Inferior function: thinking

ENFJ
The Nurturer

ENFJs love people. They have an uncanny understanding of what is important to others, and they communicate their caring concern. Happiest when they are nurturing others, they are usually able to say whatever is needed to make everyone feel comfortable. They are likely to choose work that lets them interact with others, and they are most effective when they are given plenty of encouragement and approval.

ENFJs are . . .

Expressive: their emotional reactions are usually plainly visible.

Sympathetic: they identify with others, looking for areas of agreement; they love to admire other people openly.

Talkative: they solve their problems and generate ideas by talking; in fact, they enjoy talking so much that they may have a hard time coming to the point.

Devoted: they stick up for people they admire, institutions they respect, or causes they believe in.

Idealistic: they know how things ought to be and how people ought to act. They try to live up to their ideals, but they are keenly aware of how often reality falls short of them.

Influential: they communicate well and do not hesitate to speak out in groups. They often make outstanding leaders.

Expectant: they are on the lookout for new ideas, new ways of doing things, new understandings of human nature.

Danger zones: ENFJs may close their eyes to situations and relationships that fall short of their ideals, thus denying themselves the opportunity to deal with problems. They may suffer under a load of guilt if they take the responsibility for maintaining harmony in any group of which they are a part. They may use their desire to nurture to control a relationship, or they may make loved ones uncomfortable by their idealization of them. They may give of themselves until they burn out. To nurture more effectively, ENFJs need to occasionally back off and let others nurture them.

ENFJ parents are deeply devoted to spouse and children. They feel responsible to maintain order and harmony in their homes, and they are generous with their time and money. Their homes are often social centers where friends frequently gather. They tend to be supportive of and companionable with the people they live with. They are unlikely to dominate or criticize.

ENFJ children are friendly, helpful, and responsible. Wanting others to be happy with them, they blossom when praised and wilt when criticized. They may take on more responsibility than they can handle with their limited experience, even to the point of not looking out for their own needs. They have vivid imaginations and remarkable insight about human nature. These children are often popular, both with their peers and with adults. Tending to feel that the real world never quite measures up to their ideals, they often love the world of literature, music, or art.

> Similar type: ESFJ
> Dominant function: feeling
> Second function: intuition
> Inferior function: thinking

ESTP
THE ADVENTURER

ESTPs love life and want to experience as much of it as possible. They may enjoy sports, either playing or watching. They may like machinery or mechanical things that can be used, taken apart, and put back together. They get great satisfaction from material possessions and physical experiences: clothes, furniture, and cars; fine dining, the arts, entertainment. They don't especially enjoy management, but they can be excellent in sales—or in any other kind of work that allows them to size up and respond to the need of the moment.

ESTPs are . . .

Resourceful: they are usually able to deal with whatever life sends them.

Practical: they learn better from a hands-on approach than from studying books because they always want what they learn to have a practical application.

Observant: they absorb and remember facts and details; they are keenly aware of what is going on around them.

Easygoing: typically patient and good natured, they rarely seem stressed or worried.

Charming: often with a good sense of humor, they enjoy playing to an audience.

Adventurous: they enjoy excitement and risk taking, whether in sports or in their careers.

Independent: if they think it is necessary, they may buck public opinion or sacrifice friendships for their current interest. They do not want to be fenced in.

Danger zones: In line with their sometimes daring lifestyle, ESTPs may not stop to consider possibilities for the future. If they have not developed their thinking judgment, they may make having fun their first priority. Looking for excitement, they may compromise their safety or integrity, or they may become undisciplined and lazy. They may find lasting commitments rather boring. To keep the adventure alive, ESTPs need to use their thinking judgment to check the long-term implications of their actions.

ESTP parents can be a lot of fun. They are generous, amusing, and full of exciting ideas. They enjoy introducing their children to a world of adventure; they can also share their knowledge of sports, tools, and machinery. They may, however, sometimes spend more time with their friends than with their families; and if there is a lot of tension at home, they may stay away even more. An SJ child, who needs a predictable environment, may be charmed but baffled by an ESTP parent.

ESTP children want to explore virtually everything but school (unless school gives them freedom to pursue their interests). Action oriented, they are constantly on the go. They want their pursuits to be exciting or useful, and they like to share their interests with friends. They learn by touching, tasting, smelling, and taking apart, not by studying words and diagrams in books. They may enjoy getting into mischief, especially if their natural expressiveness is blocked.

> Similar type: ESFP
> Dominant function: sensing
> Second function: thinking
> Inferior function: intuition

ESFP
THE HEDONIST

ESFPs love life and want to experience as much of it as possible. They may enjoy sports and crafts, especially if they can do them with friends. They get great satisfaction from material possessions and physical experiences: clothes, furniture, and cars; fine dining, the arts, entertainment. Their greatest interest is people. ESFPs don't especially enjoy management, but they can be excellent in sales. They are especially good at working with people in crisis.

ESFPs are . . .

Resourceful: they are usually able to deal with whatever life sends them.

Practical: they learn better from a hands-on approach than from studying books because they always want what they learn to have a practical application.

Observant: they absorb and remember facts and details, especially about people.

Easygoing: typically patient and good natured, they rarely seem stressed or worried; they refuse to look at problems.

Charming: often with a good sense of humor, they love performing.

Generous: they will give their last dime to a friend, and they do not keep accounts.

Sociable: sympathetic and warm, they enjoy entertaining and going to parties.

Danger zones: ESFPs are likely to be impulsive and may not always consider the consequences of their actions. If they have not developed their feeling judgment, they may make the joy of the moment their first priority. Looking for excitement, they may compromise their safety or integrity or become undisciplined and lazy. Feeling expansive, they may endanger their financial security. To experience life at its richest, ESFPs need to use their feeling judgment to see that their actions are in line with what they really want.

ESFP parents can be a lot of fun. They are generous, amusing, and full of exciting ideas. They enjoy introducing their children to a world of adventure; they can also share their knowledge of sports, handicrafts, and human nature. They do not usually tolerate anxiety well, however, and they may become impatient if a child falls ill or gets in trouble. ESFP parents tend to be reluctant and inconsistent disciplinarians. An SJ child, who needs a predictable environment, may be charmed but baffled by an ESFP parent.

ESFP children give a lot of themselves to virtually everything but school (unless school gives them freedom to pursue their interests). Action oriented, they are constantly on the go, and they like to share their interests with friends. They learn by touching, tasting, smelling, and taking apart, not by studying words and diagrams in books. They may enjoy getting into mischief, especially if their natural expressiveness is blocked. ESFP children are extremely vulnerable to others' beliefs and expectations, often patterning themselves after whoever they are with.

> Similar type: ESTP
> Dominant function: sensing
> Second function: feeling
> Inferior function: intuition

ENTP
THE ENTREPRENEUR

ENTPs love exploring possibilities. Anything worth doing is worth changing, and ENTPs enjoy coming up with projects, interesting other people in them, and tirelessly carrying them out. They dislike routine and are happiest when they can implement one new idea after another. When not trying something new, they enjoy tossing ideas back and forth with their associates.

ENTPs are . . .

Enthusiastic: once involved in a project, they think of little else, and they usually persuade others to join them in their interests.

Independent: they are not impressed by authority, and they never want to do anything the time-honored way.

Resourceful: because they are good at improvising, they often do not prepare well in advance—but they seem to come out okay anyway.

Innovative: they are constantly on the lookout for new procedures, new goals, new insights.

Impulsive: uninterested in long-term plans, they prefer to follow the inspiration of the moment; this leads them to many interests in rapid succession.

Analytical: they want to know *why*. They like to have

fun with logic; they are often skilled at arguing both sides of a question.

Competent: they may go to great lengths to impress others with their competence and understanding, which they value highly.

Danger zones: ENTPs may find it hard to pay attention to detail, even when it's important to their projects. If they ignore their thinking judgment, they may begin more projects than they can possibly finish, abandon them when the going gets rough, and give in to discouragement when their genius is not recognized. To make their projects succeed, they need to use their thinking judgment to limit the number they take on and to hold them to completing each one.

ENTP parents can be wonderful teachers. Enthusiastic and good natured, they can introduce their children to a wide variety of ideas and interests. Inquisitive and logical, they can motivate their children to look for causes and to predict consequences. Because they love trying new things, however, they may sometimes endanger their family's economic or physical well-being. Although they are unlikely to be harsh with their children, they may not pay consistent attention to them; the interest of the moment may lure them away from family responsibilities.

ENTP children are imaginative daydreamers who lose things, mess things up, and constantly come up with wonderful plans. They rarely use their toys the way they were designed to be used: a teddy bear can be a soldier one day and a football the next. They love to discuss issues from all points of view, even those that contradict their own. They enjoy trying to outwit the system.

> Similar type: ENFP
> Dominant function: intuition
> Second function: thinking
> Inferior function: sensing

ENFP
THE ENTHUSIAST

ENFPs love exploring possibilities. Anything worth doing is worth changing, and ENFPs enjoy coming up with projects, interesting other people in them, and energetically carrying them out. They dislike routine and are happiest when they can implement one new idea after another. Interested in other people, they work well with them and for them.

ENFPs are . . .

Enthusiastic: once involved in a project, they think of little else, and they usually inspire others to join them in their interests.

Independent: they never want to do anything the time-honored way; rather than challenging authority figures, however, they are likely to try to inspire them with their own vision.

Resourceful: because they are good at improvising, they often do not prepare well in advance—but they seem to come out okay anyway.

Innovative: they are constantly on the lookout for new procedures, new goals, new insights.

Impulsive: uninterested in long-term plans, they prefer to follow the inspiration of the moment; this leads them to many interests in rapid succession.

Idealistic: their projects often turn into causes; they may interpret their options in terms of good and evil.

Connected: having many friends and personal contacts, they enjoy connecting people with positions, information, or other people.

Danger zones: ENFPs may find it hard to pay attention to detail, even when it's important to their projects. If they ignore their feeling judgment, they may begin more projects than they can possibly finish, abandon them when the going gets rough, and give in to discouragement when their idealistic goals seem out of reach.

To make their inspirations succeed, they need to use their feeling judgment to limit the projects they take on and hold them to completing each one.

ENFP parents can introduce their children to a wide variety of ideas, interests, and people. In fact, their children may have friends all over the world! Enthusiastic and good natured, ENFPs can be fun to live with. They may confuse their children (and mates), however, by alternating extravagance and thrift or by switching attitudes midstream: one moment they are stern authority figures, the next they are friends and companions. Children who crave order and predictability will not know what to do with their ENFP parents, but they will never doubt that they are loved.

ENFP children are imaginative daydreamers who lose things, mess things up, and constantly come up with wonderful plans. They rarely use their toys the way they were designed to be used: a teddy bear can be a soldier one day and a football the next. They are interested in everything and everybody: no other type is likely to have as many wild and crazy career ideas. ENFP children love to talk, and they can often charm their way out of any difficulties they meet.

> Similar type: ENTP
> Dominant function: intuition
> Second function: feeling
> Inferior function: sensing

ISTJ
THE TRADITIONALIST

ISTJs love the traditional American virtues: working hard, saving, using common sense, keeping their word, doing it right. It is not surprising that they are among the "salt of the earth." Since they are quiet and unassuming, they are sometimes ignored or taken advantage of. ISTJs are happiest when they are doing their duty.

ISTJs are . . .

Dependable: when they say they will do a thing, you can be sure they will follow through. Their word is their bond.

Thorough: they notice and take care of details; no dirt under the rug or unfinished corners for them.

Conservative: believers in order and authority, they lend their support to traditional religion, politics, manners, and morals.

Practical: they pride themselves on common sense; they base their decisions on experience and a knowledge of the facts; and they would rather a thing be useful than interesting.

Persistent: hard workers, they do not give up when the going gets rough; instead, they work steadily until a job is completed.

Analytical: they base their opinions on logic and common sense, not primarily on personal considerations.

Dutiful: they believe in law and order, and they are willing to fulfill their obligations.

Danger zones: ISTJs believe in their own approach to life, and they have little time to spare for people whose lifestyle is at odds with theirs. If they do not accept the possibility that other attitudes, other behaviors could be valid for other people, they risk being prejudiced or judgmental. Some ISTJs are so dutiful that they forget how to have fun, and some are so sensible that they forget how to use their imaginations. If ISTJs train themselves to put themselves in the other person's place, and if they allow themselves a few wild and crazy moments now and then, they will become strong rather than brittle.

ISTJ parents are committed to their children and spouse. They are good providers, and their homes are neat and functional. They enjoy family traditions, and they take seriously their responsibility to discipline and educate their children. They keep their promises, and they are consistent. Most children benefit from their patient parenting, although a child who strongly prefers perceiving may find them too restrictive. ISTJs may seem too cool and distant to a child who prefers feeling judgment.

ISTJ children are quiet and obedient. Practical and dependable, they often do well in school. They enjoy hands-on hobbies they can do by themselves—collecting and classifying, playing a musical instrument, handicrafts. They usually don't need reminding to be on time, to do their chores, to clean their rooms. They may, however, need a little help in letting go and having fun.

> Similar type: ISFJ
> Dominant function: sensing
> Second function: thinking
> Inferior function: intuition

ISFJ
THE LOYALIST

ISFJs love the traditional American virtues: working hard, saving, using common sense, keeping their word, doing it right. It is not surprising that they are among the "salt of the earth." Since they are quiet and unassuming, they are sometimes ignored or taken advantage of. ISFJs are happiest when they are meeting their obligations to people they care for.

ISFJs are . . .

Dependable: when they say they will do a thing, you can be sure they will follow through. Their word is their bond.

Thorough: they notice and take care of details; no dirt under the rug or unfinished corners for them.

Conservative: believers in order and authority, they lend their support to traditional religion, politics, manners, and morals.

Practical: they pride themselves on common sense; they base their decisions on experience and a knowledge of the facts; and they would rather be helpful than interesting.

Persistent: hard workers, they do not give up when the going gets rough; instead, they work steadily until a job is completed.

Sympathetic: genuinely concerned with others' welfare, they are quietly friendly, tactful, and kind.

Devoted: they support and are loyal to institutions (the church, their company, the school, the community) and individuals (family members, friends, people in need) they believe in.

Danger zones: ISFJs believe in their own approach to life, and they have little time to spare for people whose lifestyle is at odds with theirs. They may be terribly upset when people do not behave as they think they should. In addition, ISFJs tend to work too hard. Wishing to please everyone, ISFJs may bottle up their negative emotions and suffer headaches or backaches as a result. To do the most good to others, ISFJs need to remember to take care of themselves, to delegate responsibilities, and to take time off now and then.

ISFJ parents are committed to their children and spouse. They are good providers, and their homes are usually attractively decorated and well kept. They enjoy family traditions, and they take seriously their responsibility to discipline and educate their children. They keep their promises, and they are consistent. Most children benefit from their patient parenting, although a child who strongly prefers perceiving may find them too restrictive. Occasionally an overworked ISFJ may play the martyr.

ISFJ children are quiet, obedient, and affectionate. They need strong relationships, and they are steadfastly loyal to their parents and siblings. Practical and dependable, they often do well in school. They tend to enjoy being helpful, and they may like jobs with tangible results: baking cookies, polishing silver. They usually don't need reminding to be on time, to do their chores, to clean their rooms. They may, however, need a little help in letting go and having fun.

> Similar type: ISTJ
> Dominant function: sensing
> Second function: feeling
> Inferior function: intuiting

INTJ
THE STRATEGIST

INTJs love coming up with new systems, new theories, new understandings—and then translating them into reality. Naturally organized and highly determined, these are people whose faith can move mountains. They are happiest when they have new mountains to move and when they can clearly see that their goals are in sight. Many INTJs work with such apparent ease in the external world that their associates do not realize they prefer introversion. Because of their ability to achieve the impossible, they are often given executive positions.

INTJs are . . .

Original: they are always on the lookout for new angles, new interpretations, new possibilities for understanding the world and efficiently controlling it.

Pragmatic: although they love theory, they want their ideas to work, to be accepted, and to be useful.

Decisive: they make decisions easily and organize their projects efficiently.

Determined: sometimes stubborn, they are capable of single-minded concentration until their ideas are worked out in reality.

Logical: they use logical analysis to check the value of ideas, whether their own or others.

Critical: skeptical, they question everything, sometimes forgetting to be tactful.

Independent: they do not bow to established authority or public opinion; they trust their inspirations and pursue them without help, if necessary.

Danger zones: INTJs may be so persuaded of the value of their goals that they overlook formidable obstacles and opposition. Tending to reject contrary opinions, they may miss the advice they most need to hear. Many INTJs are uncomfortable in social situations, and their own relentless efficiency may cause others to fear them. This further isolates them from the feedback they need. To achieve their remarkable goals, they need to stay open to input from their sensing and from other people.

INTJ parents are dedicated and supportive. They often give their children the independence they crave for themselves, allowing them to follow whatever paths they choose. They tend to be fair in their discipline, and their children respect them. The children may, however, be a little afraid of them, since INTJ parents can be hard to figure out. If approached when their minds are on their work, they may seem hurried; often without meaning to, they seem emotionally distant.

INTJ children almost raise themselves. They do not want interference with their projects, and they do not need reassurance that they are on the right track. In fact, they do not respond positively to praise unless they think it is deserved. These children often plan well ahead, sometimes making decisions before they have adequate information. They tend to be high achievers at school, even though they daydream a great deal.

> Similar type: INFJ
> Dominant function: intuition
> Second function: thinking
> Inferior function: sensing

INFJ
The Oracle

INFJs love coming up with new ideas, new theories, new understandings about people—and then using them for the common good. Naturally organized and willing to do whatever is needed to make their dreams come true, these are people whose faith can move mountains. They are happiest when they see their insights helping others. Many INFJs work so apparently comfortably with others that their associates do not realize they prefer introversion. Because of their clear goals, skill at working with people, and willingness to work hard and long, they may be put in executive positions. They often prefer, however, to work behind the scenes.

INFJs are . . .

Original: they are always on the lookout for new angles, new interpretations, new possibilities for contributing to the welfare of others.

Pragmatic: although they love theory, they want their ideas to work, to be accepted, and to be helpful.

Decisive: they organize their projects efficiently and with concern for their colleagues' well-being.

Persevering: they are capable of single-minded concentration until their ideas come to fruition.

Sympathetic: they like to please others, and they dislike conflict. They work well with people on a one-to-one basis.

Imaginative: with vivid awareness of their inner reality, they may be drawn to poetry, mysticism, or psychic phenomena.

Sensitive: keenly aware of others' needs and also of their own, they are likely to be easily hurt.

Danger zones: Some INFJs are so persuaded of the value of their goals that they overlook formidable obstacles and opposition. Ignoring unpleasant truths, they may leave out the data they most need to include. Other

INFJs, torn apart by conflict and criticism, give up good ideas rather than face the opposition. Thus a tendency to want only positive feedback can make INFJs pursue unworkable projects or abandon good ones without cause. To do the greatest good for the greatest number, they need to learn to examine negative input but ignore it if it does not apply.

INFJ parents are strongly devoted to their children. They pay close attention to all aspects of the children's development: physical and emotional health, mental and spiritual growth. They often praise their children and enjoy being friends with them, even though they also discipline them firmly. Sometimes they tend to encourage their children to be overly dependent on them.

INFJ children are often quiet and dreamy. They want to understand others and themselves, and they want to be understood, but they are uncomfortable if asked to open up when they are not ready. If they are close to a parent, they may talk for hours about what is important to them. Or they may write—journals, poetry, stories, songs. They may have vague ambitions to help humanity in some grand but unspecific way. These children often plan well ahead, sometimes making decisions before they have adequate information. They tend to be high achievers at school.

> Similar type: INTJ
> Dominant function: intuition
> Second function: feeling
> Inferior function: sensing

ISTP
THE EXPLORER

ISTPs love having the freedom to learn *why.* Intensely independent, they don't care much for regulations, authority figures, or public opinion. They are happiest when they can use their abilities in order to understand the world—perhaps by analyzing data or by taking apart intricate machinery. They tend to do their work thoroughly and well, whenever and however they please.

ISTPs are . . .

Cool: they enjoy working alone on the job and at their hobbies; they also enjoy team sports that don't require a lot of talk. Except with their closest friends, they are usually shy.

Exacting: when they make something, everything fits together smoothly; when they analyze data, their figures are correct.

Analytical: they are interested in the logic behind machinery, statistics, or the natural world.

Inquisitive: wanting to know about cause and effect, they like to stand back and ask why.

Independent: they do not happily accept authority and restrictions, wanting to be left alone to do their own thing.

Impulsive: whether at work or play, they do what they want, when they want. They are drawn to excitement; they enjoy doing things other people would call risky.

Manually adept: they are often knowledgeable about and skillful with tools and weapons.

Danger zones: Not fond of either talking or writing, ISTPs may have a hard time communicating their insights to others. They may alienate people close to them by criticizing them more often than praising them. In addition, ISTPs tend to dislike binding obligations. If they take their love for freedom too far, they may find themselves out of work or in trouble at home. To gain the freedom they crave both at home and at work, ISTPs need to train themselves to consider how their words and actions affect others. With others' support, they will be given much more latitude than without it.

ISTP parents like to do things with their children— playing touch football in the back yard, climbing mountains, fixing the leaky roof. Engrossed in such an activity, they may enjoy talking with their children. Never of their own choice, however, will they sit down with them—or anyone else—for the sole purpose of having a chat. ISTP parents are not dictators. They don't enjoy disciplining their children or forcing them to do things they don't enjoy. If the children put up a fuss, ISTP parents are likely to withdraw to their workroom.

ISTP children want to know *why*. If they ask, they will listen carefully to logical explanations. More likely, they will try to find out for themselves by direct investigation. Quiet and usually orderly, they use their toys as the toys were intended to be used—although they may take them apart first to see how they are constructed. These children are obedient if they think the rules are fair; otherwise they quietly go their own way.

> Similar type: INTP
> Dominant function: thinking
> Second function: sensing
> Inferior function: feeling

INTP
THE PHILOSOPHER

INTPs love having the freedom to learn *why*. Intensely independent, they don't care much for regulations, authority figures, or public opinion. They are happiest when they are gathering ideas, insights, and theories; they enjoy analysis for its own sake. Rigorously logical, they are likely to prefer jobs involving research over those requiring communication or administration.

INTPs are . . .

Reserved: having learned that most people don't understand their ideas anyway, they reserve conversation for their closest friends.

Precise: in thought and words, they are consistent, concise, and coherent; they intensely dislike sloppy thinking.

Analytical: analysis is their tool for unlocking the mysteries of the universe, and only logical reasoning will persuade them to adapt or discard an idea.

Inquisitive: intellectually curious, they read widely and observe carefully in their attempt to learn as much as possible.

Independent: in relating to others, they happily live and let live—although under no circumstances will they give up their cherished principles and understandings.

Creative: they are fertile in ideas, quick in understanding, ready with solutions to intellectual problems, and full of insights.

Theoretical: their interests are rarely practical or personal; their chief interest is understanding the principles behind natural, divine, or human law.

Danger zones: Not interested in simplifying the profound truths they like to think about, INTPs may have a hard time communicating their insights to others. They may alienate people close to them by criticizing them more often than praising them. In addition, INTPs tend to lose themselves in theory, forgetting to check their perceptions against external reality. If they do this, they may waste their abilities in the pursuit of the impossible or the impractical. To gain respect for their insights and to promote peace at home, they should learn and practice principles of effective communication.

INTP parents are devoted to their children, although they may seem preoccupied a good deal of the time. They are generally easy to live with, but they get uneasy if the home atmosphere is chaotic. Usually they feel more comfortable around children who are old enough to talk intelligently than around babies and toddlers. They tend not to be demonstrative in their affections, and they are likely to be oblivious to family traditions, including birthdays, unless they are repeatedly reminded.

INTP children want to know *why.* If they ask, they will listen carefully to logical explanations and try to poke holes in answers that do not hang together. More likely, they will try to find the answers for themselves, either by reading or by thinking the problem through. INTP children may be so lost in thought that they are oblivious to their surroundings a good deal of the time. If this is the case, they are likely to suffer a lot of teasing. They may not relate well to other children, or they may simply prefer their own company. These children are obedient if they think the rules are fair; otherwise they quietly go their own way.

Similar type: ISTP
Dominant function: thinking
Second function: intuition
Inferior function: feeling

ISFP
THE SPRITE

ISFPs love working behind the scenes to contribute to valued persons or causes. They are happiest when they are working individually at something that matters deeply to them, and they get deeply involved in work they feel is important. They enjoy the moment, and they take great pleasure in sensory experiences. Because they are usually very quiet and often underestimate their own worth, they are often overlooked or misunderstood at school, at work, and even at home.

ISFPs are . . .

Reserved: quiet and retiring, they show their warmth and enthusiasm only to their closest friends.

Idealistic: they have strong values that influence every aspect of their lives—work, homes, friendships.

Self-deprecating: they demand a great deal of themselves, and they often feel that they do not measure up.

Gentle: not interested in obtaining power or position, they prefer to follow and support.

Compassionate: they care deeply about family,

friends, the less fortunate, and those who suffer.

Attentive: they are content to work alone and for a long time, paying close attention to detail.

Sensory: highly aware of sense impressions, they may be interested in music, dance, food, clothing, or the visual arts.

Concrete: rather than expressing their feelings in words, they do so through loving deeds or beautiful creations.

Danger zones: ISFPs may demand too much of themselves or expect too much of the world. They feel disappointment keenly and may be vulnerable to depression. If they neglect maintaining healthy contacts with the world, they can become unrealistic. If ISFPs lose sight of their interests and goals, they may drift from experience to experience. To be filled with the warmth and beauty for which they hunger, ISFPs need to filter their goals and interests through a screen of realistic common sense, rejecting the unwise and impossible and pursuing those where they have a good chance of being effective.

ISFP parents are likely to be kind and sympathetic. Although they do not talk much, they often have an instinctive rapport with babies and toddlers. They love doing things for their children. They may take special joy in family holidays, because then they can show their love through gift giving, decorating, and meal preparation. Children who enjoy nature—gardening, animal care, romps through the woods—will be especially blessed if they have an ISFP parent.

ISFP children are gentle, cheerful, and lovable. They also may seem mysterious and even breakable because of their introversion and their sensitivity. More interested in making or experiencing things than in speaking or writing about them, they may have trouble adapting to school routines. They blossom, however, in a relatively free atmosphere where they know they are appreciated and loved.

Similar type: INFP
Dominant function: feeling
Second function: sensing
Inferior function: thinking

INFP
THE VISIONARY

INFPs love working behind the scenes to contribute to valued persons or causes. They are happiest when they are working individually at something that matters deeply to them, and they work long hours when they feel their work will make a difference. They often lose sight of the present moment in their zeal to improve the future. Always looking for perfection, they are likely to be appreciated by others more than they appreciate themselves.

INFPs are . . .

Reserved: quiet and retiring, they show their warmth and enthusiasm only to their closest friends.

Idealistic: they have strong values that influence every aspect of their lives—work, homes, friendships.

Self-deprecating: they demand a great deal of themselves, and they often feel that they do not measure up.

Gentle: not interested in obtaining power or position, they prefer to follow and support.

Compassionate: they care deeply about beloved persons and causes.

Focused: they like concentrating on their work but will pay attention to details only if they are directly related to their area of interest.

Curious: always interested in possibilities, they welcome new ideas and insights.

Verbal: they are usually good at expressing themselves, especially in writing.

Danger zones: INFPs may demand too much of themselves or expect too much of the world. They feel disappointment keenly and may be vulnerable to depression.

They don't mind bypassing logic and ignoring present reality, and this can lead them into impossible crusades. To make the world a better, purer, kinder place, INFPs need to consult with people of different personality types before raising the standard and calling the troops to battle. With a clear view of reality, INFPs can set the world on fire.

INFP parents are likely to be deeply committed to their children and spouse, perhaps turning their families into one of their personal causes. They are easy to live with, sympathetic, and devoted to their family's welfare. They may, however, suffer from a nagging sense that the reality of their daily life does not measure up to their vision of what could—and should—be.

INFP children are thoughtful and eager to please. Even as small children they have delicate consciences. They know what is right, and they try to do it. They want others to do it, too—but they also want to maintain family harmony. INFP children are fortunate indeed if they have a parent who listens to, understands, and encourages their idealism.

Similar type: ISFP
Dominant function: feeling
Second function: intuition
Inferior function: thinking

BIBLIOGRAPHY

Books

Brownsword, Alan. *It Takes All Types!* San Anselmo, Calif.: Baytree Publication Company, 1987.

A readable introduction to type that combines Myers's type theory with Keirsey's temperament theory. Especially helpful for someone who wants to teach others about type, because the presentation is unusually clear and well organized.

Faucett, Robert and Carol Ann. *Personality and Spiritual Freedom: Growing in the Christian Life Through Understanding Personality Type and the Myers-Briggs Type Indicator.* New York: Doubleday Image, 1987.

A readable introduction to type that focuses on spiritual growth, emphasizing one's relationship to self, to others, and to God. Includes reflection questions.

Golay, Keith. *Learning Patterns and Temperament Styles: A Systematic Guide to Maximizing Student Achievement.* Fullerton, Calif.: Manas-Systems, 1982.

Of interest to elementary school teachers, this book applies temperament theory to learning styles, classroom environment, curriculum and instruction, and teacher-student relationships.

Grant, W. Harold; Thompson, Magdala; and Clarke, Thomas E. *From Image to Likeness: A Jungian Path in the Gospel Journey.* New York: Paulist Press, 1983.

Presenting the theory that psychological type develops gradually over the course of a lifetime, these Catholic authors show the spiritual strengths of all four functions.

Jung, C. G. *Psychological Types.* The Collected Works of C. G. Jung, vol. 6, Bollingen Series XX. Princeton, N.J.: Princeton University Press, 1971.

Since the MBTI is based on Jungian theory, specialists may wish to read Jung himself. Because Jung deals primarily with pathology and addresses himself to an academic audience, this book is recommended for professionals who already understand psychological type.

Keirsey, David, and Bates, Marilyn. *Please Understand Me: Character and Temperament Types.* Del Mar, Calif.: Prometheus Nemesis, 1978.

This well-known book about temperament theory shows how four temperaments (based on MBTI types) influence leadership style, learning patterns, childhood development, and other areas.

Kroeger, Otto, and Thuesen, Janet M. *Type Talk: How to Determine Your Personality Type and Change Your Life.* New York: Delacorte Books, 1988.

A comprehensive introduction to type theory with applications to work and relationships. Contains extensive profiles of the sixteen types.

Lawrence, Gordon. *People Types and Tiger Stripes: A Practical Guide to Learning Styles,* 2d ed. Gainesville, Fla.: Center for Applications of Psychological Type, 1982.

Written for teachers by a professor of education, this book is also full of practical help for parents. The author describes the types clearly and provides practical tools for working with children of different types. Includes an early version of Myers's *Introduction to Type*.

Mamchur, Carolyn Marie. *Insights: Understanding Yourself and Others*. Toronto: The Ontario Institute for Studies in Education, 1984.

An imaginative and sometimes whimsical introduction to type theory. The author takes pains to introduce the concepts in terms that each type will appreciate. Includes many verbal and photographic illustrations.

Michael, Chester P., and Norrisey, Marie C. *Prayer and Temperament: Different Prayer Forms for Different Personality Types*. Charlottesville, Va.: The Open Door, 1984.

Valuable descriptions of the ways people of differing temperaments relate to various forms of prayer. May seem a bit foreign to Protestant readers, but for that reason may provide challenging new insights.

Myers, Isabel Briggs. *Introduction to Type: A Description of the Theory and Applications of the Myers-Briggs Type Indicator*, 4th ed. Palo Alto, Calif.: Consulting Psychologists Press, 1987.

If you didn't get a copy of this booklet when you took the MBTI, write for one now. It should be the first thing you read when learning about psychological type.

Myers, Isabel Briggs, and McCaulley, Mary H. *Manual: A Guide to the Development and Use of the Myers-Briggs Type Indicator*. 2d ed. Palo Alto, Calif.: Consulting Psychologists Press, 1985.

For professional users of the MBTI, this large book

is invaluable. In addition to explanations and applications of type theory, it includes a wealth of statistical tables summarizing research on psychological type.

Myers, Isabel Briggs, with Myers, Peter B. *Gifts Differing.* Palo Alto, Calif.: Consulting Psychologists Press, 1980.

Of all the readable books on psychological type, this is the most comprehensive and accurate. Written by one of the developers of the MBTI, it includes chapters on marriage, early learning, occupation, and type development. Highly recommended.

Page, Earle C. *Looking at Type: A Description of the Preferences Reported by the Myers-Briggs Type Indicator.* Gainesville, Fla.: Center for Applications of Psychological Type, 1983.

Another introductory booklet, even more basic than *Introduction to Type,* using cartoons to explain the preferences. Very helpful in understanding type and in explaining it to others.

Von Franz, Marie-Louise, and Hillman, James. *Lectures on Jung's Typology.* Dallas: Spring Publications, 1971.

Von Franz gives helpful information about the inferior function, but her presentation is quite academic. Recommended only for the professional who already has a good grasp of psychological type.

Journals

Journal of Psychological Type.

Subscriptions from Thomas G. Carskadon, Ph.D., Editor/Publisher, Department of Psychology, P. O. Drawer PF, Mississippi State University, MS 39762. Published twice yearly, this is the official research journal of the Association for Psychological Type. Single copies available from CAPT (see below).

The Type Reporter.

Subscriptions from Susan Scanlon, Editor, 524 North Paxton Street, Alexandria, VA 22304. Published four times a year, this is a popularly written magazine looking at practical aspects of psychological type and temperament.

Other Resources

Note: Publishers and distributors are permitted to sell the Myers-Briggs Type Indicator and the Murphy-Meisgeier Type Indicator for Children only to qualified professionals. For information on professional training required and where it can be obtained, call any number below.

The Association for Psychological Type, P. O. Box 5099, Gainesville, FL 32602 (904/371-1853).

Membership organization for people interested in psychological type. Membership benefits: newsletter, journal, membership directory, national and regional conferences, training program. APT's local chapters sponsor talk groups where members can share observations about type.

Center for Applications of Psychological Type, 2720 NW 6th Street, Gainesville, FL 32609 (904/375-0160 or 800/777- CAPT).

Distributes, for professionals and the public, books, training materials, research reports, and MBTI and MMTIC testing materials. Provides basic and advanced professional training for applications in counseling, education, and religion;

also provides research consultation and services, computer scoring services, and the Isabel Briggs Myers Memorial Library.

Consulting Psychologists Press, 577 College Avenue, Palo Alto, CA 94306 (415/857-1444).

Publishes many psychological tests, including the MBTI and the MMTIC. Distributes testing materials and related books.

Otto Kroeger Associates, 3605 Chain Bridge Road, Fairfax, VA 22030 (703/591-MBTI).

Management consulting firm dealing with MBTI. Distributes books related to type theory; provides training seminars and workshops for families as well as businesses.

Type Resources, Inc., 9525 Georgia Avenue #206, Silver Spring, MD 20910 (301/585-8855).

Distributes testing materials and books related to type theory; provides training, consulting, and counseling services.

GLOSSARY

Attitude: Extraversion or introversion. Tells where you prefer to focus your energy—on the outer world of people and things, or on the inner world of concepts and ideas.

Auxiliary function: The function (S or N, T or F) that works with your dominant function to give you balance. Introverts use their auxiliary function in the external world; extraverts use it in the internal world. Also called "second function."

Dominant function: The function (S or N, T or F) that you developed first, are most comfortable with, and use in your preferred world (external or internal).

Extraversion: The attitude of being more at home in the external world of people and things than in the internal world of concepts and ideas.

Feeling: The judging function that makes decisions based on deeply held values and ideals.

Function: One of four psychological processes that all people use all the time: sensing, intuiting, thinking, and feeling.

Inferior function: The least developed of the four functions (S or N, T or F) and the polar opposite of the dominant function.

Introversion: The attitude of being more at home in the internal world of concepts and ideas than in the external world of people and things.

Intuition: The perceiving function that takes in information about the world through imaginative leaps and association of ideas.

Judging: The orientation of running one's outer life through a judging function, either thinking or feeling. Characteristic style: decisive and well planned.

Judging functions: Thinking and feeling, the two functions used for making decisions and acting on information received.

MBTI: The Myers-Briggs Type Indicator. A well-researched, standardized, validated instrument for assessing psychological type.

MMTIC: The Murphy-Meisgeier Type Indicator for Children. Similar to the MBTI, the MMTIC is used with children ages 7-12.

Orientation: Judging or perceiving. Tells whether you prefer to conduct your outer life by planning or by adapting.

Perceiving: The orientation of running one's outer life through a perceiving function, either sensing or intuition. Characteristic style: relaxed and adaptable.

Perceiving functions: Sensing and intuition, the two functions used for gathering information.

Sensing: The perceiving function that takes in information about the world through close attention and careful observation.

Temperament: A way of grouping similar types. In this book we look at Keirsey's four temperaments: SJ, NT, NF, and SP.

Thinking: The judging function that makes decisions based on logical analysis and firm principles.

Type: A distinct personality pattern. In this book we look at the sixteen psychological types identified by the MBTI (see the appendix for a separate discussion of each type).